Contents

Acknowledgments   vii

Preface   ix

Introduction   1
Why is it so daunting?   2
Why is it worth doing?   3
How is this book going to help?   4
What basic assumptions guide this book?   5
Won't we just get stuck?   6

1. Involving Others   8
Students   9
Parents, board members, graduates   12

2. Teaching and Leading   16
Empowering teachers   19
Promoting growth in all adults   19
Supporting and encouraging collaboration   20
Spreading ownership   23

3. School Culture 24
What constitutes school culture 24
Characteristics of successful schools 26
Tumultuous Prep 28
Ourtown High School 28

4. Overcoming Barriers 30
Approaching the hurdles 32
A case in point 33

5. Time and Schedule 35
Finding the time 35
"The schedule won't allow it" 37

6. Broadening Horizons 40
Research 41
A crucial distinction 44
Clarifying exercises 47

7. The Hidden Curriculum and the Null Curriculum 51
The hidden curriculum 52
The null curriculum 55

8. Sample Process for Curriculum Review 58
Seeing the need 60
Getting started 62
Self-examination: determining what you have 64
Research: broadening horizons 66

Paths to
New Curriculum

Stephen C. Clem
Z. Vance Wilson

National Association of Independent Schools
75 Federal Street
Boston, Massachusetts 02110

ABOUT THE AUTHORS . . .

Stephen Clem worked in independent schools for eighteen years as a French teacher, department head, and head of upper school. He has been at NAIS for five years as associate director and director of academic services. As staff liaison to the NAIS Academic Services Committee, he has been involved in the committee's curriculum project from the beginning.

Vance Wilson is a writer and a teacher. He was an English teacher, coach, and principal at the Lovett School (Ga.) and English chair, dean of faculty, and writer-in-residence at The Asheville School (N.C.). He wrote *They Took Their Stand*, a nonfiction account of the integration of Southern independent schools. He has also written a novel, *The Quick and the Dead*, and short stories.

Library of Congress Cataloging-in-Publication Data
Clem, Stephen C., 1946–
    Paths to new curriculum / Stephen C. Clem, Z. Vance Wilson. p. cm.
    Includes bibliographical references.
    ISBN 0-934338-73-6
    1. Curriculum evaluation—United States. 2. Education—United States—Curricula.
I. Wilson, Zebulon Vance. II. National Association of Independent Schools. III. Title.
LB 1570.C55   1991
375'.006'0973—dc20   90-29122
                                        CIP

Goal setting: determining what you want   67
Implementation and evaluation: making
  things happen   68

**9. Coherence, Complexity, and
   Interdependence   70**

10. Questions for Curriculum Review   73
Seeing the need   74
Getting started   76
Self-examination: determining what you have   78
Research: broadening horizons   83
Goal setting: determining what you want   88
Implementation and evaluation: making
  things happen   89

Resources   93
Books   94
Professional associations   102
Government-associated agencies and institutes   104

Acknowledgments

A community of educators created this book.

Teachers and administrators from across the country have for years volunteered their time and effort for the schools the National Association of Independent Schools serves. One such group of volunteers is the Academic Services Committee. Although the topic of curriculum had been on the committee's agenda for many years, in 1987 we began to envision a curriculum review project that would require a sustaining focus unusual for committees, both from those members who would rotate off before the project was completed, and from those who would be asked to join in the effort when they began new terms.

In 1988 the committee tested for interest by surveying NAIS member schools about curriculum and curriculum review. An unusually high number of schools responded, with almost all of them expressing interest in a process of review that would serve schools. The committee was of course pleased with the survey results but immediately ruled out any idea of defining a core curriculum in favor of studying new ways schools could review their current curriculum and set about improving it. Not surprisingly, we gained a new respect for the challenge facing schools as eleven committee members and four NAIS staff people tried to step out of their own deeply held convictions and watch themselves argue, question, try again, and keep on task in search of a final manuscript. We wrote seven drafts, which says much about our stylistic flaws but more about the process of educators trying to agree about curriculum review.

Acknowledgments

The following people either wrote, edited, critiqued, or researched part of this book: Dory Adams, Dulany Bennett, Robert Blair, Hope Boyd, Jim Buckheit, Janet Edwards, Bill Ellis, Preston Hannibal, Tim Johnson, Karen O'Neil, David Mallery, and Dorothy Strang.

We would also like to thank Art Powell, Susan Stone, and Grant Wiggins for sharing their expertise with us during discussions about curriculum and process in the last three years.

Over the summer of 1990 we sent a draft to educators across the country. They gave us invaluable criticism, from overall impressions to diction. And they encouraged us not to give up. We owe great thanks to Phineas Anderson, Brenda Aronowitz, Earl Ball, Joyce Ferris, Brother Thomas Frerking, Linda Hennelly, John Mason, Cathy Meisel-Valdez, Dennis O'Neil, Suzanne Perot, Charlotte Rea, and Linda Wilson. Special thanks also to Richard Black of NAIS for his work on the manuscript and to John Esty, president of NAIS, for his encouragement and support.

Steve Clem and Vance Wilson are listed as authors of this book because we gathered together everyone else's writings, notes, and comments and tried to stitch them into a narrative. For their encouragement in our work, we also thank our families.

Preface

In the mid 1960's, when I was head of The Taft School, in Watertown, Connecticut, I appointed a faculty committee to review the curriculum. I was dismayed—but not too surprised—to discover that they needed several months just to get oriented, to find appropriate resources, to develop a way of proceeding, and even to figure out what questions to ask. I knew schools of education had undergraduate majors in "curriculum" and that hundreds of doctoral dissertations had been written on the subject. I knew there was a time when the old Independent Schools Education Board talked a lot about curriculum, and the early NAIS conferences had whole workshops on the subject. But I had no idea that the gap between public school theory and practice of curriculum development and what we did in independent schools had grown so great.

Now, at long last, with the appearance of this new NAIS book, that gap has narrowed—or at least the weakness of independent school practice has been addressed. Borrowing from the best of public school experience and drawing on a survey of several hundred independent schools, the authors, with the help of the NAIS Academic Services Committee, have produced what they call "a model process for the evaluation and review of curriculum."

But this book is more than a guide to curriculum development: it is a wise, thoughtful, experienced, and data-based commentary on how schools work. Chapters 1 through 7 invite school professionals, including board members, to learn more about the heart of their school's culture and operation. These chapters also provide a way to decide whether to take a sharp look at the curriculum and why. The resource list at the end of the book, alone, would have saved the Taft School review committee scores of hours,

We think this short volume is worth a quick reading by every school head and chief academic officer, and perhaps the chair of the board's academic committee. Certainly it should be required reading for every member of the curriculum review committee.

I congratulate the authors and their supporting committee for a notable contribution to strengthening the process by which an independent school—or any school—decides what to teach and why.

John C. Esty, Jr.
President, NAIS
Winter 1991

Introduction

But to change the curriculum involves more than changing a text or two, a course or two. Behind, and within, the curriculum is a long, complex cultural, intellectual and political tradition. We must consider the multiple contexts of the curriculum if we would understand what we wish to change in more than a narrow, superficial way. . . .

Old knots and tangles that are in all our minds and practices must be located and untied if there are to be threads available with which to weave the new into anything like a whole cloth, a coherent but by no means homogeneous pattern.
— Elizabeth Kamarck Minnich, *Transforming Knowledge*

Every school, whether public or nonpublic, has a "curriculum," with some defining it narrowly as the collection of texts used in different subjects at different levels. Others take a broader view that encompasses pedagogy and outcomes and activities outside the classroom. Still others find no agreed-upon definition of what curriculum is and is not.

Nevertheless, something called "the curriculum" is in place in all schools, and changing that monolithic entity can be particularly daunting, especially in the day-to-day press of events, like trying to unload and reload a moving train. So daunting, in fact, that many schools never get beyond a kind of piecemeal, "let's fix what's broken" approach.

Why is it so daunting?

All change is threatening.

It follows, then, that thinking about curriculum change is threatening. The mere mention of curriculum review suggests changing what we teach and how we teach it and, at least by implication, who teaches it; at that level, anyone might get nervous. No wonder that schools can get "stuck" when they think about curriculum. Yet how can we not think about it?

Even for the best-intentioned and the least anxious the barriers seem legion.

- Sometimes it's people. One school struggled for years to revise its offerings in history in order to be more inclusive, but change always seemed impossible. But when the long-time head of the department retired, it was easy to change the program.

- Sometimes it's the schedule. Another school's desire to offer more interdisciplinary courses in the middle school foundered on the rocks of a schedule constrained by cross-over teachers and limited gym space.

- Sometimes it's internal structures. Overly rigid departmentalization can polarize curricular discussion, creating battles for turf and leading to passive—if not active—resistance to even the smallest changes. And virtually any change can be successfully resisted and even sabotaged.

- Sometimes it's history. The "we tried this before and it didn't work" response can be a powerful roadblock in any institution as long-time veterans—and not without reason—remind colleagues of past false starts and frustrations. Often a simple recitation of all the different names of committees that have tried to talk about curriculum will suffice to paralyze real inquiry.

- But always it's time. Dedicated and committed school people get so busy that even ordinary meetings feel like a burden, and the thought of more meetings to tackle curriculum review, especially given all the other obstacles, can be terribly discouraging. But what an irony to be caught up in a curriculum that so absorbs our energy that we can't even find the time to reflect on what we're doing.

The good news is that you can overcome these barriers, thoughtfully review your curriculum, and make the changes that seem appropriate and necessary. The review process can be energizing and exciting.

Why is it worth doing?

Given the anxiety, the complications, and the time commitment necessary, why should a school, a teacher, or any group of educators choose to look hard at curriculum?

Curriculum review, when carried out thoughtfully, yields enormous benefits that more than justify the time and energy needed.

- Students are better educated.

- Educators feel re-energized, challenged, validated, and more connected to one another and the school's mission. Much of the current reform movement in education argues for giving teachers more of a say in curricular decision making.

- The school's constituencies learn to collaborate and gain new insights into one another's perspectives.

- When adults in the school take the time to reflect on, evaluate, and change what they are doing and how they do it, they provide a powerful role model for students.

- Everyone becomes more comfortable with the future and the change needed to prepare for that future.

- The school, better able to articulate its mission and program, is thus better able also to differentiate itself from the other public and nonpublic schooling choices available to parents.

How is this book going to help?

When NAIS surveyed schools in spring 1988 about current practice in curriculum review, we discovered that many schools that had set out to look at their program were frustrated by constraints of time and the lack of a useful process to follow. For want of a better tool, many schools used the occasion of an accreditation review and the accompanying materials to look at their curriculum. Because the review involved in accreditation tends, of necessity, to be descriptive of the status quo, many found that that exercise was not fruitful enough.

As the Academic Services Committee of NAIS discussed these results, we realized that the best thing to do was to help schools by providing a model process for the evaluation and review of curriculum. We set ourselves the task of designing an approach that would be flexible enough to allow for different kinds of schools, different approaches to curriculum, and reviews of different scope.

This book offers resources for further study, addresses obstacles openly and suggests ways to eliminate them, raises important issues, recognizes what schools are really like as well as what they might be, and argues for self-awareness, broadening horizons, inclusiveness, connectedness and collaborative decision making.

What basic assumptions guide this book?

Like any school faculty, the members of the Academic Services Committee brought to the topic of curriculum review a multiplicity of opinions and preconceived ideas. Early on we recognized that we had to ask ourselves what we believed about curriculum and curriculum review.

We offer these assumptions not as a definitive list to constrain or inhibit your own discussions but, rather, to be honest with you about our agenda. You may agree with some of our assumptions, disagree with others, or want to define ones that we have left out. We believe that any curriculum review needs to flow from, and be informed by, clearly stated assumptions or beliefs. Here are some.

- Curriculum is best defined as all the experiences children have under the guidance of teachers and/or school. This view considers almost anything in school, even outside school (so long as it is planned).

- The primary goal of any curriculum review is to provide students with a better education.

- Teachers take the central role in transforming and implementing curriculum.

- Curriculum review is challenging and sometimes painful.

- Planning and implementation of curriculum must be conscious, deliberate, and open.

- Curriculum content and pedagogy are inextricably linked. Curriculum planning must examine both.

- Curriculum and curriculum planning are inherently political and never value-free. Making the underlying values of curriculum explicit is crucial. We believe, for example, that curriculum and pedagogy should specifically address and seek to correct race, ethnic, gender, and class bias.

- Establishing the goals and values of a school's curriculum should include representatives of the school's major constituencies.

Defining assumptions is challenging work and not the way we usually do business in school. We want to jump in and fix things and then move on to something else, feeling that we don't have time for "philosophical" discussion (and what does it mean that "philosophical" has become, somehow, pejorative?). Hammering out your assumptions is messy: people will talk, agree, disagree; get excited, get angry; change their minds, reach clarity, lose clarity; work for consensus, dig in their heels; give, take, and then want to talk some more. But this is where you have to start.

Throughout the process, from the planning stages to implementation and assessment, you must give yourself time for extended discussion. Every single aspect of successful curriculum review builds from a working definition of curriculum and a list of assumptions the people in the school share. Above all, don't be discouraged by disagreement; the alternative to dialectic is a stale status quo. If a conflict can be satisfactorily resolved, the process by which the resolution is gained will profit the review and the school culture. And if it can't be resolved, that will highlight important divergences in the school community that must eventually be addressed. Clarifying points of contention and then working to resolve or reconfigure them may well be the most productive parts of your review.

Won't we just get stuck?

Only if you let it happen.

We don't endorse endless, circular, fruitless discussion, the confusion of pointless talking with doing. Haven't we all been involved in groups whose discussions went on and on with no results until finally the school year ended or the group simply ran out of energy and never met again? Don't those memories make us cringe when someone says, "Let's form a committee and look at X, Y, and Z"? One school principal was even heard to say, "Our curriculum committee lasted longer than my marriage."

It doesn't have to be this way. There are no mysterious, inexorable forces that condemn groups to staying eternally stuck. Groups often get stuck and stay stuck because of an unspoken but powerful consensus that moving ahead is just too risky. Real commitment, strong leadership, honesty, and clear goals will keep you moving.

Curriculum transmits messages of all kinds; the modes of transmission are messages themselves. The right messages in school, clearly heard and fully embraced, can transform a student's life. Of course, the old messages are no longer the only messages. We must recognize our myopia about the rich diversity of cultures in our country and our deep biases about race, gender, and class. We should be trying to redefine our messages to include these new understandings, even though we aren't yet exactly sure what the messages should be. This redefinition means examining what we teach and how we teach it. Doing the job well means studying, talking, listening, deciding, and implementing. This book is meant to help in these efforts.

1.
Involving Others

The students in good . . . schools feel visible and accountable. They balance the pulls of peer group association with the constraints of adult requirements. And they embrace the tensions between the utilitarian promises of schooling and the playful adventures of learning. — Sarah Lawrence Lightfoot, *The Good High School*

One school dropped its seventh grade Latin requirement in order to create an interdisciplinary humanities program but neglected to keep parents and graduates informed and involved. They found themselves in the middle of a firestorm of protest and spent a year dousing the flames, their best energy diverted from implementing the new program. Another school adopted an exciting new lower school math program after considerable study, but encountered extraordinary resistance from parents who found it hard to help their children with their homework. Special meetings and workshops finally helped bring people around, but time and momentum were lost.

The school's professional educators are the key players in any curriculum review, and Chapter 2 addresses the roles they must play, but no review can be truly successful if the school's other constituencies are not part of the process. Identifying, involving, and honoring those constituencies is a vital early step in thinking about curriculum review.

Students

We struggle with who students are, but we try to describe them. We stand before an audience, stare at a screen, write notes to ourselves, all the time searching for the proper metaphor. Students are our masters. Students and their parents are our clients, to whom we should market a top-of-the-line product. Students are the clay for our potter's hands; let us mold them into responsible citizens. And, though we seldom speak this metaphor, we often think of students as patients whose diseases, called childhood and youth, we diagnose and cure.

And then, when a single metaphor doesn't work, when "masters," "clients," "clay," and "patients" remain inadequate, we search through vague language having to do with vocation. We say, "Students are what it is all about," implying that "it" means our lives, our vocations, our schools, and even our future. A teacher at a faculty meeting says, "Why are we in this profession if not for the students?"

Students don't always want to help us, don't want to be the figures in our rhetoric. Some pass through school, from pre-K to cap and gown, guessing what we want them to say in order to keep us from finding out who they are. All too often, when we try to describe who students are, we deceive ourselves into believing they are who we were as students, or—more nearly—the way we remember ourselves.

A school reviewing its curriculum begins by looking at its people: administrators, teachers, the school board or board of trustees, graduates, parents, and students. From the beginning a curriculum review tries to keep clear each group's individual and collective identity, but since five out of six of these groups are composed of adults, they have more power or, at least, more access to power. They have traditionally defined roles and great skill at articulation; they seldom lose influence on the process. Students are often neglected, either by seldom being mentioned in curricular discussions or, more likely, by being neatly sealed off in the school's philosophy.

A school must examine its assumptions about students and the curriculum and, if necessary, change its priorities. This means listening to students and working to help them become agents of their own education. Students do not make final decisions about what the curriculum should be. They are not, after all, professional educators, but they are professional consumers and can learn to be thoughtful users and critics of what is happening in the school.

If students are as important as every school's language says they are, involve students in critiquing their own education. Ask them what courses they have been engaged by, ask them how what they have learned in a history class has helped them outside of class, ask them if a middle school science class has shown them how to experiment. Ask them about pedagogy. Do they feel comfortable with lectures, and do they know what part of a lecture is important enough to put in their notes? Do they prefer working alone, with a partner, or in small groups? What methods of invention and revision best work for them in writing? What kind of classroom environment do they prefer?

As important as actual questions is the way we listen. We sometimes give lip service to involving students by placing the token student or two on a committee. This does not lead to understanding who students are, nor does it involve more than a few students in their own education. Some individual teachers seek "feedback" about their classes in a variety of ways, such as essays, evaluations, and interviews. Some schools track their students' learning by placing writing samples and selected art-work in folders at the end of the year. These serve as marvelous portraits of a student growing. What if, in an attempt at more global feedback, the school at certain checkpoints interviewed all students about the curriculum? This might show how the school's intentions and the students' experiences match up.

Another way to find out what it is like to be a student in your

TRY THIS . . .

Consider asking your students some of these questions—or make up your own.

☞ What interesting connections have you seen among the ideas you have studied?

☞ Describe how you learn best.

☞ What work has really engaged you?

☞ What is the best way to set up a classroom?

☞ What kind of feedback helps you learn?

☞ How would you restructure the school day? The school year?

☞ What are some of the questions that interest you?

☞ How effectively do you communicate your ideas and beliefs?

☞ Describe good teaching. How do you know it when you see it?

☞ Draw a picture of the school with yourself in it.

☞ How has the school made a difference in your life?

☞ Tell me about someone here at school who has been important to you.

☞ What do you like about school? What might we do differently?

☞ What opportunities have we not offered you?

☞ How is this school a good place for you? A not so good place?

☞ Write me a letter this summer about how the year was for you.

☞ What have you learned about yourself?

☞ What are your hopes for the years to come? How can this school help you?

☞ What do you want to learn next week? next year? How do you want to learn it? How will you know that you have learned it?

☞ What do we seem to value here, through word and deed and more subtle messages?

school is to have every member of your curriculum planning group shadow a student for a day or two (but not in their own division or grade level) and keep a journal. Then share those journals with one another. Or have someone you respect and trust from outside your school shadow a student.

Finally, what are the outcomes you wish for your students? What do you wish them to be and to know at certain points in their time with you? What should be the results of all that time spent in your company? Working backwards and forwards from the answers will help you decide on appropriate curriculum and pedagogy.

DON'T FORGET!

If you believe that talking to students at all grade levels to get their opinions of the school's curriculum is a good idea, do it now. And think about how to make this conversation part of the way you do business.

Parents, board members, graduates

Although parents and board members are not direct "consumers" or practitioners of curriculum, they are deeply invested in what happens in the school and can be particularly sensitive to change. They are all stakeholders. Not to involve these people, in appropriate ways, in curriculum review and change is to court disaster.

In the second quotation at the beginning of the chapter, another price was paid for exclusion: an erosion of trust among those constituencies. All the apologies, backtracking, and educating could never really erase the sense, for those people who felt excluded, that the schools didn't take them seriously or, at least, were not interested in their perspectives. Feelings like these linger in groups, get passed along, and tend to resurface for years.

The most important perspective is that these other constituencies need to be included, not just to head off problems, but also because they will enrich the process itself, bringing different views and different priorities to bear on crucial curricular questions. No curriculum plays itself out in a vacuum; what happens in the classroom expands through space and time as students move

TRY THIS . . .

Here are some questions to keep in mind as you consider curricular change.

☞ What are our constituencies? Who are the formal and informal leaders of those constituencies?

☞ Who in these constituencies will be confused about the possible changes? How can we educate them?

☞ Who will grieve (the word is not too strong) over what's lost? How can we acknowledge those feelings and help them see what has been gained?

☞ Who will be excited and eager to help? How can we enlist them as our allies, liaisons, and spokespeople?

☞ Who might be angry? What can we do to bring them along? And what if they can't be brought along?

☞ Are we clear enough ourselves about what we are doing so that we can explain it convincingly? (Change always has to be "sold" to almost everyone.)

☞ What research supports our ideas? How can we share it?

☞ How can we best communicate what we are doing? What vehicles will we use?

☞ How will we honor the past and celebrate change?

☞ How will we monitor and evaluate the reactions of the different constituencies as changes unfold?

through the school. The experiences and outlooks of parents, students, and graduates are vital for the school's deliberations.

Trustees and school board members, of course, have responsibility for the school's mission and overall educational program, as implemented by the principal or head of the school, and most boards have an education committee that works with the head and others to give broad direction to the school's curriculum. Including board members in whole-school review is logical and usually happens. If they are not actively involved in reviews of smaller scope, it is important to keep them apprised of the evolution of your thinking, perhaps through reports to the education committee or through the head.

Involving others is not as easy as it sounds. Just talking about involving others—even students—in curriculum discussions can make people very edgy. Our first reaction, as trained professionals, is often, "What do they know about curriculum? Or teaching? Or scheduling?" Is there any teacher or administrator who hasn't felt, at least once, the fight-or-flight response when confronted by a parent or board member who has challenged, however gently, what was happening in the classroom, division, or school? Not to mention how it feels when they are not gentle.

But involving others is crucial. That is not to say that we give any single group veto power over decisions—boards, of course, already have it—but rather that the attitude and process be such that the school or review group is constantly seeking to include

---

DON'T FORGET!

Involving others in a curriculum review not only improves the quality of the review but is an action that should have broader positive ramifications for the whole community. You can start right now creating ways to be sure that all the voices in your school are heard.

---

others, to educate them, and to enlist their support. We must carefully define the role of others and communicate that definition clearly. Including others makes the process itself better and guarantees better results in both the short and the long run. And by its actions the curriculum review group models the best way to make decisions that stay made.

2.
Teaching and Leading

Teaching and leading are distinguishable occupations, but every great leader is clearly teaching—and every great teacher is leading.
— John W. Gardner, *On Leadership*

When teachers close the door they become the curriculum.
— Alan Glatthorn, *Curriculum Renewal*

When the best leader's work is done, the people say, "We did it ourselves." — Lao Tzu

Here's an experiment to try: go around your school and ask people if they consider themselves to be leaders in the school. Chances are that very few will say, "Yes, I am." People in schools feel that there is something antidemocratic, presumptuous, and maybe even threatening about identifying themselves as leaders. Even people formally identified as leaders may find it hard to claim that title and will search for other descriptions: "I really see my job as supporting the work of the teachers," or "I'm just here to serve the students."

Equally difficult is getting people to say outright that someone else is the leader. Doing so seems to suggest that we need something we can't supply ourselves, that we are in some way incomplete or insufficiently motivated. And yet when things aren't going well we will quickly proclaim, "What we really need is some strong leadership." But when we get it, sometimes we are sorry we asked. Working through this ambivalence is critical, because curriculum review must have effective leadership.

This ambivalence has repeatedly surfaced in our efforts to create this book. On the one hand, we want realistically to acknowledge that, while building community requires consensus and collaboration, different positions with different amounts of power exist within schools. Each position also has different responsibilities. A school head might seek assistance in almost every aspect of his or her job, but final authority in certain crucial decisions can rest with no one else.

On the other hand, we strongly believe that effective curriculum review can happen only when "teachers take the central role in transforming and implementing curriculum" (see our assumptions in the Introduction). Only when the school culture endorses both collaborative decision making and a fearless exchange of ideas can the school make lasting progress. In as many instances as possible, teachers should lead and leaders teach; most important, they should do so together.

Consider two examples of effective curriculum reform.

A second grade teacher and her kindergarten colleague next door initiated a long-term multi-age classroom project almost inadvertently when, one day, a troublesome second grade boy found what he needed for himself in the block corner of the kindergarten room. Recognizing that this discovery was also a fortuitous event for them, in ways that extended far beyond keeping the boy doing the same thing for an hour, the two teachers began to plan a joint venture. Materials previously reserved for one class were combined with those reserved for the other class. Walls were eventually knocked down. When appropriate, students of different ages were mixed together.

The venture ended up lasting ten years, and at its height it involved six teachers sharing a common space. They could not have succeeded in their venture, of course, without the support and encouragement of the officially designated leaders of the school. The principal found them time to work out the idea and space to put it into practice. The principal also insisted that they read enough theory to ground their practice, a requirement they initially resisted but came to appreciate as they explained and justified their new classroom to colleagues, parents, and visitors. The energy and insight of these teachers were not lost behind closed doors, and they produced good results for the school because an atmosphere of cooperation and learning existed among colleagues in different positions.

In a high-tech, business-oriented community that was home to a diverse population, a school head was asked repeatedly whether the school had considered teaching Japanese. When rumor of such an idea spread among the parents, the school head began receiving calls asking whether the school was going to drop Latin. Then other parents asked whether starting French 1 in the seventh grade and not receiving high school credit for the work was wise policy. This school head was sensitive to the parents' concerns, believing that all three issues were important, but he knew as well that making one choice— adding Japanese to an overloaded curriculum, dropping Latin, or moving French 1 to the eighth grade for credit—was not what the school needed. It also didn't need him to make each of these decisions in isolation and then announce the new curriculum to the faculty.

What began was a long and thorough review, guided for the most part by teachers, of foreign language study throughout all the grades of the school. The head created a schoolwide committee and asked its members to enlist the assistance of the local university and the regional association of foreign language teachers. The head also insisted that the study last a year in order to be thorough. From the beginning the head was involved—he was leading—but he also recognized that curriculum review could not be effective if it were done piecemeal and if the enactors of the curriculum, the teachers, were not instrumental in making the necessary decisions.

How does a school create an environment where, though lines of authority are clear, teaching and leading overlap in a creative and productive way? There are four crucial tasks: to empower teachers, to promote growth in all adults, to support and encourage collaboration, and to spread ownership.

Empowering teachers

Citing Diane Common's article "Power: The Missing Concept in the Dominant Model of School Change" in his book *The Empowerment of Teachers*, Gene Maeroff writes,

> Reforms fail because the teacher is cast in "the role of the user rather than creator of curriculum ideas and materials. The ensuing power struggle between the reformers who would impose top-down change on the teachers rather than letting it come from the teachers ends up producing no change at all." Teachers in effect have veto power in instances where they do not have the power to implement. This kind of power is basically negative. Were teachers truly empowered and accorded a key role in determining curriculum, then substantial changes might result.

Lee Shulman, in his work in teacher assessment at Stanford University, makes the same point when he distinguishes between "curriculum as mandated" and "curriculum as enacted"; curriculum review that does not accord teachers a key role will ultimately fail. The research points in one direction: toward teachers as decision makers and enactors.

Promoting growth in all adults

To act in a way that benefits students and the community requires that those who are empowered continue to mature as adults. Isolation among the adults in a school restricts growth. In *Promoting Adult Growth in Schools*, Sarah Levine addresses this crucial cultural issue.

> The organizational structure of most schools separates adults within self-contained classrooms. Physical separation can also mean social,

psychological, and professional isolation. Yet peer interaction is a key component of school improvement; likewise, it is an essential aspect of adult development.

Both the teacher isolated in his classroom and the administrator isolated in her office need peer interaction within the confines of the school, in the community, and in a professional development context such as further schooling, conferences, and workshops, to name only a few possibilities. A curriculum review that encourages all adults in the school to become fully engaged, to seize the initiative, to develop a sense of purpose, and feel a part of the decision-making process will at the same time underline the essential nature of a school's development program for both teachers and administrators.

Supporting and encouraging collaboration

In his book *On Leadership* John Gardner suggests that leaders must

- Envision goals

- Affirm values

- Motivate

- Manage

- Achieve a workable level of unity

- Explain

- Serve as a symbol

- Represent the group externally

- Renew

Each verb suggests different constellations of qualities and skills. None is the province of only one position in a school. None must necessarily be cloaked in authority. Gardner points out that leadership is needed from all positions in a school and that it can also come from teams of people.

Who will be your leaders? How will you collaborate? Different tasks and circumstances call for different leaders and styles. The key leadership roles in a curriculum review should be defined according to talent and not necessarily by title. In many schools, an experienced teacher is asked to coordinate a school's self-study in preparation for accreditation, bringing fresh insight and under-employed skills to bear on this important task.

Leadership can also come from those in administrative roles. In a schoolwide review, the head or principal must be completely engaged as one of the leaders and is probably the best person to shape the initial goals and supply the necessary momentum.

In addition, a curriculum review may have its own leaders while the group, collectively and individually, provides leader-ship for the rest of the school community. Leadership and collabo-ration are not mutually exclusive concepts; in fact, real, productive collaboration is nurtured by strong leaders, whose effectiveness is symbiotically enhanced by collaboration. And sometimes it takes strong leaders to get people to start to collaborate: a school whose culture sanctions competition, subtly or overtly, will not readily embrace collaboration; the win-lose paradigm is tenacious and used to getting its way.

Specifically, curriculum review leaders must

- Believe in the possibilities for a creative and useful review.

- Articulate the need for curriculum review and promote its potential benefits for all.

- Focus on the broad view, especially in a whole-school review.

- Overcome barriers.

Teaching and leading

- Help each constituency and individual to see how the pieces weave together into a single, integrated fabric.

- Model openness to feedback and change.

- Forge and encourage connections.

- Value and reward experimentation and risk taking.

- Honor and resolve conflicts.

- Help groups work well.

- Obtain logistical and financial support for curriculum review.

TRY THIS . . .

☞ Interview the faculty and staff in your school. Ask them who the leaders are.

☞ Identify those teachers and administrators who have successfully worked for curriculum change in the past. Ask them how they saw their own roles in those changes.

☞ Describe the most successful curriculum changes in the school's past decade. What leaders helped make those changes possible? How many of them were classroom teachers? What style of leadership was most effective?

☞ Evaluate your professional development program. Does it help the adults in your school learn to share power and collaborate in decision making?

☞ Describe important curriculum changes led by people who are no longer at your school. Have the ideas embodied in the change outlasted the people who imagined them?

Spreading ownership

Finally, it is important to recognize and reflect on the mistake schools often make of having a part of or even all of the curriculum depend upon a single person: "We will teach a new course only because Mr. Smith is here to teach it," or "We can incorporate music into the morning activities only because this school head is here to push the idea into action." What happens if a key person in your curriculum plan leaves? School people are moving to new places with increasingly frequency.

No matter how important certain people are to the effective running of a school, curriculum is the responsibility of everyone, both in the present and in the future. If an idea can't outlast us, it can't really succeed.

> ### *DON'T FORGET!*
> Think about implementation at each stage of a curriculum review. Even though you may not yet have clear goals, you can probably anticipate some of the challenges, and you can certainly begin preparing people to cope with the stress and emotions of change. And if a new idea is born from the curriculum review, implement it now.

3.
School Culture

It is in and through education that a culture, and polity, not only tries to perpetuate but enacts the kinds of thinking it welcomes, and discards and/or discredits the kinds it fears.
— Elizabeth Kamarck Minnich, *Transforming Knowledge*

The differences between Tumultuous Prep and Ourtown High School are not all that noticeable within the confines of algebra class. Students may well be using the same book, and teachers may be members of the same math teachers' consortium at the local university. Even the students' scores on national exams could well be similar. Yet anyone who knows the two schools will tell you they are very different. The differences between Tum and OHS are not so much a function of curriculum as they are a function of the two schools' "cultures."

What constitutes school culture

In order to review its curriculum well, a school must take an inward look and know itself. Culture is an amalgam of formal and informal symbols and structures, and written and unwritten rules, the "who we are–how we do it–what makes us special" part of a school. A school's culture is usually quite distinctive, but it is not always easy to articulate. And culture is also often expressed in the school's hidden curriculum and null curriculum (see Chapter 7 for more on these phenomena).

School culture is not necessarily captured in the school's mission statement or its logo. On a school's letterhead may burn the lamp of learning, but the most significant attribute of the school may instead be the strict discipline people believe the recently retired principal embodied. Another school may boast a well-articulated organizational chart illustrating lines of authority and the process by which decisions are made, but the structure that really matters could be informal—the alliance of senior faculty members at a certain lunch table. Often neither the school's mission statement nor the school's organization and rules have the efficacy and power of the unspoken agreements that govern the social system: who talks—or at least gets listened to—at faculty meetings; what books are sacrosanct; whether secretaries are treated as colleagues; whether the rules about student conduct in the halls are enforced by everyone.

Although schools seldom openly discuss such examples of real power, all of them suggest that culture determines how power is distributed and exercised. At the senior faculty lunch table, the fifth grade teacher convinces his colleagues, before the meeting of the curriculum committee, not to integrate the language arts curriculum with the middle school. Or the head, an Anglophile, rules against the English department and insists that American literature students stop studying Twain and Dickinson and Henry James in the middle of the year to read *Macbeth*, "for a child," he explains, "must be exposed to Shakespeare at least once a year." And, because only the dean of students enforces school rules in the hallways, students learn that the adults in the school believe that proper behavior doesn't matter unless it directly affects their authority in class.

At the heart of the matter, these political arrangements—these issues of power—may dictate the extent to which the curriculum is viewed as a collection of independent, autonomous parts (divisions or disciplines) or as an integrated whole.

The ability of a school to review and change its curriculum will depend upon a key dynamic in the school culture: the ways the school encourages separateness or connectedness.

Characteristics of successful schools

Jon Saphier and Matthew King, in "Good Seeds Grow in Strong Cultures," identify twelve characteristics of the culture of successful schools.

- Collegiality
- Experimentation
- High expectations
- Trust and confidence
- Tangible support
- Reaching out to the knowledge base
- Appreciation and recognition
- Caring, celebration, and humor
- Involvement in decision making
- Clean procedures
- Traditions
- Honest, open communication

The greatest challenge facing a school is building a sense of connectedness within the organization and creating an ethos of

TRY THIS . . .

As you prepare to review your school's curriculum, consider Saphier and King's characteristics of a successful school's culture and ask yourself these questions.

☞ What is the nature of collegial relationships in the school?

☞ How does the school show its willingness to experiment?

☞ Are there expectations for every member of the community? What are they? How do people know what is expected? What happens when expectations are unmet?

☞ Do people trust one another? Have confidence in one another?

☞ What tangible support systems are in place? Do they work?

☞ How does the school demonstrate its commitment to learning?

☞ How do people know they are appreciated and their accomplishments recognized?

☞ How does caring manifest itself in the school?

☞ How is power distributed in the school? Is the distribution rigid? fluid? Do people have a common understanding about this distribution?

☞ Who lacks power?

☞ Is there a sense of humor about the school?

☞ What and how does the school celebrate?

☞ How are people are involved in making decisions? Who gets left out?

☞ Are the procedures of the school clearly outlined and followed? How do they get changed? What principles underlie these procedures?

☞ What traditions are important? Why? How do those traditions inform the school's culture? How do new traditions evolve?

☞ How does the school's culture support or inhibit open and honest communication?

evaluation and openness to change. Both are crucial: people may connect only to protect the status quo, and disconnected people never get or give any helpful feedback. Teachers and administrators should be colleagues who talk to one another, trust one another, and celebrate their accomplishments. Students should be trusted, recognized, given high expectations, and listened to. Everyone should understand how decisions are made. In fact, everyone needs to understand and work on articulating the school's culture and how it informs what happens.

The following scenarios sketch out what happens to the process of curriculum change in two different schools—the one clinging to separateness, the other forging connections.

Tumultuous Prep

Tum's experience with curriculum change is typical of schools with high levels of bureaucracy and separateness and little openness to evaluation and real change.

Old curriculum (before)	New curriculum (after)
Unexamined assumptions	Same unexamined assumptions
Pedagogical habits	Unchanged pedagogical habits
Philosophy as rationalization	New rationalizations
Rigid departmental boundaries	Boundaries intact
Little contact among teachers	No discussion of new elements
Syllabus in a file drawer	New syllabus in a file drawer

Ourtown High School

OHS had a different experience, possible in a school that was developing flexible structures and a high level of connectedness and trust.

Old curriculum (before)	New curriculum (after)
Unexamined assumptions	New assumptions, questioning attitude
Pedagogical habits	New methods
Philosophy as rationalization	Philosophy as criterion for evaluation
Rigid boundaries between departments, divisions	Schoolwide networks, barriers down
Little contact among teachers	Active dialogue, feedback, and support
Syllabus in a file drawer	Syllabus on the desk, in the air
	Ongoing evaluation and change
	Everyone feels ownership
	New student outcomes

Changing a school's curriculum in a lasting way may first require changing the culture. It is also true that the review process itself may help to transform the school in ways hard to imagine at the outset. Working toward connectedness and openness is the key.

DON'T FORGET!

If we can halt the daily grind and find creative ways to think about our school culture, we are taking the first steps to recognizing what is good and change what is not. And, while auditing a school's culture is important to creating an outstanding curriculum review, taking action to improve aspects of the school culture does not have to wait on a final strategic plan. If you discover, for example, aspects of your culture that are isolating or excluding, work on them immediately.

4.
Overcoming Barriers

He saw the problem before him as plain as a map. The fantastic thing about war was that it was fought about nothing—literally nothing. Frontiers were imaginary lines. There was no visible line between Scotland and England, although [the battles of] Flodden and Bannockburn had been fought about it. It was geography which was the cause—political geography. It was nothing else. . . . The imaginary lines on the earth's surface only needed to be unimagined. The airborne birds skipped them by nature. How mad the frontiers . . .
— T. H. White, *The Once and Future King*

Our perspective is often mired in the trenches. The curmudgeon who says "We did all of that curriculum stuff before, and look where it got us" looms on the horizon like a dragon whose fire will torch all our efforts. "Why try?" we ask, having lived with the curmudgeon. The admission officer who assures us that our proposed curricular change will ruin the school's reputation in the community is as intimidating as an iron fortress with its drawbridges up. "Why knock?" we ask, knowing who has the queen's ear.

If a thoughtful review of curriculum implies change, then the barriers we face in trying to pull ourselves out of the mire are many and high. Let's begin inside a school. Problems of school culture were discussed in the last chapter; time and schedule are discussed in the next. But there are more than enough problems left to muddy the landscape.

A school's curriculum has its own history. Although that history is valuable, intransigent members of the faculty and administration sometimes hallow it to the point of revising it into a myth. But the longevity of the curriculum does not of necessity mean it is good or that it is appropriate to the school's current population. Curriculum should continually be subjected to rigorous scrutiny, one that does not take "We've always done it that way" or "In the old days, we . . ." as a definitive answer.

Then there's turf. One of the unspoken agreements that exists among autonomous divisions in a school, or departments in middle and upper or high schools, is a kind of collusion—I'll stay off your turf if you stay off mine. And individuals create their own burgeoning kingdoms and make all their decisions on the basis of how many new fiefdoms they can add to their flag. Turf isolates teachers and divisions and departments from one another and makes any curriculum review have to slog in the trenches instead of moving up to new perspectives. Everyone knows turf defenders.

What about the "next level up" on the academic treadmill? Colleges get the most publicity. "We can't teach that course," someone will say, "because the colleges won't count it." Or "I don't care what it is. We've got to call it social studies, or the colleges won't pay any attention to it." The "next level up" syndrome, which applies to all levels in our education, has been such a pervasive force in the last twenty years that even our kindergartens are now academic, and our preschoolers are prepped for kindergarten admission tests.

There are still more barriers: the bias that private school people have against educational theory and research and teacher training; the board of trustees; parents; the state department of education; our school's reputation in the community; money. The list is painfully endless.

What, then, must we do?

Approaching the hurdles

Here are some suggestions for ways to begin to overcome barriers and to keep them overcome.

Try to change perceptions. Begin with turf—the issue of autonomy. "Autonomy" properly means being a lawgiver unto oneself—doing what is rational and correct without having to be told. It does not imply isolation within the walls of a classroom, an office, or in the middle of a distant playing field, or license to teach what one pleases any way one wants to. This has to be emphasized so that isolation and license will not be rationalized in the name of academic freedom.

Build trust in the school. Everyone should understand the difference between building trust and establishing agreement and between achieving commitment and winning compliance.

Eliminate boundaries between people. We create far too many divisions—between administrators and teachers, for example, without even pausing to reflect that an administrator who doesn't teach a class can still be an exceptional teacher of adults within a community and of students in a larger context, and that a teacher may very well be an exceptional administrator both in and outside the classroom. We often do not realize that we also create a boundary between teaching and learning; the school that recognizes that students are teachers and teachers learners establishes a connectedness that does much for trust and self-review.

Consider the physical environment. Elementary school teachers are often the ones who best understand the relation between physical environment and learning. In one corner is a rug where children sit and talk when they first come to class. Tables stand nearby for cutting and pasting. In another corner science experiments ferment under alphabet mobiles.

Reward vision. Any curriculum review should reward those citizens of the school who do a great job in their own bailiwick but also see beyond it and contribute to the learning that takes place not just in classrooms but everywhere in the school. Reward citizens who build trust and work for connectedness.

Finally, know the facts, especially about scheduling and college admission. Don't believe consultants who would assure you that their research shows that 85 percent of schools are using a schedule similar to the one that will work for you. A week's worth of telephone calls can bring to your school an array of scheduling possibilities from all over the country. Decide what you want to teach and how you want to teach it before you worry about when. A scheduling conflict is not a myth, but there is nothing more depressing than an educational institution driven by a computer.

A case in point

Barriers can be overcome. As Peggy McIntosh says, "Are you going to let phantom authority tell you what to do?"

In the 1980's one school re-examined its mathematics curriculum. The head of the reviewing committee carefully read the National Council of Teachers of Mathematics standards and decided to investigate the possibilities of a senior course in discrete mathematics. Visiting some nearby colleges, she found that the mathematics professors thought the course an exceptionally good idea. They argued that the majority of high school students would use the probability and statistics and even the linear algebra in their chosen field of study far more than anyone would use calculus, even though for years calculus had been considered the flagship of mathematics departments around the country.

The college counselor at the school objected. "If it doesn't have the word 'calculus' in it, then it won't wash," he said. The counselor went so far as to enlist the help of a few of the college admission officers at the same colleges the review committee chair had visited. These admission officers were quoted as saying that the discrete mathematics course could not be as significant as calculus and therefore would not help these seniors get into the college of their choice. Parents sided with the college counselor, and the course was not offered that year.

The next year, however, the review committee marshaled more facts and brought together the admission people and mathematics professors from the same colleges. Having everyone in the same room helped to break the impasse, and the college admission officers had to listen to what their own faculty members were saying.

There are facts, and there are perceptions of the facts. You have to deal with both.

DON'T FORGET!

Finding ways to overcome barriers might be the most painful part of the curriculum review process. Remember that barriers do not obstruct planning: a curriculum committee can sit in a conference room and plan forever. Barriers obstruct implementation. Talk them through honestly and reflect on strategies that might change the way people think and allow for productive action. The head of the school must be involved in thinking through these plans. Be clear about rationale, involve as many people as possible in directing the curriculum review, have the head be a part of it, then act. Don't lose courage.

5.
Time and Schedule

Time is on my side. — Mick Jagger

I'm late, I'm late, for a very important date.
— The White Rabbit, *Alice in Wonderland*

In the survey of curriculum review practices in NAIS schools, people identified time—or, more precisely, the lack of time—as the greatest obstacle to curricular change. No doubt that the people in schools, adults and children, often feel and are "flat out," with no time for yet one more thing. No doubt, either, that time is finite, at least within the boundaries of a school day, week, or year.

But it's not that simple.

Finding the time

Albert Camus said once that you could make your life seem longer by spending much of it sitting on a hard chair in your dentist's waiting room. We've all been in meetings that can make you believe in eternal life. Not only can time pass faster or more slowly, but sometimes we do seem to find more of it. The seemingly inflexible limits of the day or week become suddenly elastic with the right combination of energy, commitment, and motivation. Most of us can only wonder at those who seem to do it all and more: the newly converted jogger who "makes" two hours a day for her run; the colleague who has just finished his second novel; the friend who, we discover, works twelve hours a week at a local shelter for the homeless; or that pair of teachers who develop a new course during lunch periods. Somehow our emotions and attitudes affect our perception of time.

Given a finite amount of time and the phenomenon by which attitude governs our perception of time, those responsible for planning significant curriculum review of any scope must do two things if the process is to be successful.

Planners must allot real, measurable time to the process. To gain this kind of time, planners must be released from something else. Aside from the time itself, the gesture is a powerful symbol of the importance of this work and confers value on the outcomes. This might mean relieving people of some teaching, coaching, or supervisory duties for the duration of the project. It could also mean hiring substitutes or aides to allow the group to take off whole days together. Another idea is to schedule people in such a way that they have extra and common free time during the day. If the time is simply "added on," the deck is stacked against success.

Planners need to be able to make optimal use of planning time. The planning group should be so constituted, empowered, and supported that its members have the commitment and energy to make the best possible use of the time they have. The people are crucial, and they need to know that the institution values their work.

Planners must do both of these things. An unmotivated group with lots of time produces nothing of value. An inspired group without sufficient time only ends up being frustrated.

"The schedule won't allow it"

Then there is the schedule—that thing, that monolith, that seems to shape the life of our schools, that says "no" much more than it says "yes," and that, once up and running, is unstoppable: "We can't do that, the schedule won't allow it." For the uninitiated the schedule is bewildering and intimidating, at once a mighty fortress and a house of cards. Even for the schedulers themselves the schedule can have a life of its own: once the givens are established—double science periods, no gym on Thursday, the part-time teacher who only works mornings—and the first few "singletons" are scheduled, everything else takes on a kind of terrible inevitability.

Whatever else it is, the schedule is the outward and visible sign of the school's curriculum. If time is the true currency of schools, then the schedule is the salary scale, and a very public one at that. Any review of curriculum must be aware of scheduling strategies and constraints, not to constrict debate, but rather to ensure a common appreciation of the school's realities.

Discussing the following assumptions about curriculum, curriculum review, and the schedule may be helpful.

- Curriculum must drive schedule.

- Significant curriculum change almost always means schedule change.

- The schedule must be seen as a tool of curriculum implementation, not as the Procrustean bed onto which the curriculum is forced ("Sorry, that seminar can only have thirty-eight minutes.").

- The schedule can be changed, but it takes leadership, imagination, and will.

TRY THIS . . .

☞ You have just been asked to be part of your school's curriculum review process. What will you stop doing? (You can't say "Nothing!") What could someone else do? What doesn't really need to be done at all? What can really only be done by you? What is your favorite thing to do? Is it the most important thing you do? If you went on sabbatical, wouldn't the school get by, even though no replacement could do all you do?

☞ List five ways your schedule serves your school. List five ways your school serves the schedule.

☞ You are an anthropologist. Someone hands you your school's schedule and nothing else. Draw ten conclusions about what this exotic culture values. If you need more distance, have a friend mail you her school's schedule.

☞ Schedule as salary scale: Who makes the most "money" in the school? Who makes the least? Justify the differences.

☞ Why haven't you changed your schedule in the last five years?

☞ Now, what are the real reasons?

☞ Describe the attitude toward time that seems to dominate your school. Who sets that attitude?

☞ For a day, pay attention to how people in your school talk about time. What words do they use?

☞ Ask five students about time. If you don't like what you hear, remember who structures their day (and much of their evening) and provides their models.

- Those responsible for scheduling must be a part of the curriculum review process, acting as key consultants, not as final arbiters of what does or does not "fit." Curriculum review is much more likely to succeed if the schedulers feel some ownership of the changes.

- Scheduling constraints are real, but schools can sometimes change reality according to the priorities they define. And sometimes reality can't be changed.

- Significant scheduling changes can almost never be made by consensus, because some people, rightly or wrongly, will see themselves as "losing" in the new configuration. At some point, someone may have to say "This is what we are going to do."

- There comes a time when people have to try something new, even if they don't want to. Rewarding these leaps of faith is important.

Other barriers to good curriculum review and change exist. Ignoring time and schedule are two of the highest ones, making it hard to succeed.

DON'T FORGET!

Creating time for people to work on a curriculum review is perhaps the single most important action you can take. To work with time in a positive way is to model behavior that makes change possible.

6.
Broadening Horizons

Educational theorizing seeks to understand and depict meaningful human action for the purpose of guiding practice.
— Noreen B. Garman, *School-Based Professional Development*

Say that every year you and your friends make a trip from A to Z and the trip always takes three days. By now you know the roads so well you could probably make the drive in your sleep (and maybe you already have). A new bridge has gone up so that, if you took it, it would save you six hours of driving and put you on a new and much more scenic route. If you're not actively looking for new routes, if you never get a new map, if you never talk to people who also go to Z, you never find out about the new way. Of course, you'll still get to Z every year, but haven't you and your passengers lost something?
— Steve Clem

W hat to teach and how to teach are the two most important decisions schools make, yet often they are made in a vacuum or in small, idiosyncratic pieces that create no coherent whole. This chapter argues for not making decisions in a vacuum. Any curriculum development process should be linked to a research base. Whether or not a particular piece of research turns out to be useful or cogent, a school needs to know what's "out there ."

Think about how we advise students about making important decisions, such as where to go to college. First of all, we ask them to start thinking about it seriously more than a year before they actually have to say yes to a college. We tell them next that they need to take a thorough and honest look at themselves and be able to articulate their goals, their strengths and weaknesses, and their needs. After this personal and intellectual inventory comes the crucial phase of research, finding out all they can about a wide range of colleges; a student's initial list might well contain twenty to thirty schools. We encourage them to think broadly at this stage, to find out what's out there, not to limit themselves to the schools they have heard of or their parents went to or their neighbor thinks would be just right for them. It's axiomatic: by casting a wide net, they will make a better decision.

The list gets narrowed, and then there are visits, applications, and essays. Students think and write and write some more, constantly asking for advice and reactions. And then, in the spring, they finally choose their college. The point all along has been to gather knowledge in order to make for the best possible match between school and student.

Why is it, then, that a school sometimes makes curricular decisions without casting a wide net, without finding out what the best thinking is on a given topic, without doing the research it believes in so completely in almost every other endeavor?

Research

Teachers really do believe in research. Think, for example, of the individual teacher's painstaking endeavor to get a lesson or a unit just right. A middle school history–English team reads a dozen novels set in revolutionary America before choosing one for joint study, and the director of a choir for a newly constituted age group polls all the area choir directors for pieces he can do with changing male voices. An upper elementary school teacher rounds up "resources" of as many different kinds as possible to fill the room before her students start their research on Mexico.

And what about administrators? Alumni/ae officials read newspapers and magazines from across the country and abroad; development officers spend hours researching the biographies of the school's graduates; admission officers comb through demographic studies and surveys; and school heads study all the research other administrators have produced, and more.

Why can't we channel some of this abounding energy for research to the whole curriculum?

Granted, among all the research, some of it seems irrelevant, and much of it seems contradictory. And there never seems to be enough time to keep up with it.

But in reality no individual or faculty can be up on all the latest research on child development, teacher effectiveness, learning theory, learning disabilities, school organization effectiveness, gender equity, multiculturalism, cooperative learning, and everything else. But every possible effort, both individually and schoolwide, should be made to learn more.

Here are some strategies an individual or a school can pursue.

- Study the resources section at the end of this book and choose some articles and books to read.

- Consult the closest school of education for professors who can speak articulately about educational trends either to a large group or serve as consultants to an individual or a small group.

- Consult college academic departments for information on what is needed for further study in the field.

- Try curriculum specialists. They usually have a great deal of training and information, have more time allocated for keeping up with professional reading, and may understand the realities of schools and classrooms better than many education researchers or professors.

- Focus the use of the school's professional development resources (money and time) on furthering teachers' knowledge of new developments in education.

- Find individuals in your own school who are expert in certain areas of curriculum and invite them to speak or lead discussion groups.

Being familiar with the current state of knowledge in one's field is the hallmark of a true professional. In "Teachers and Professionalism," Jon Moline defines the "paradigm professional" as someone who "has a mastery of a specialized body of knowledge and who is part of a professional community which autonomously and collectively establishes standards for its own work." Establishing this kind of community in a school can only enrich faculty lives, making teachers feel stronger in their vocation. It also provides for the students a model of adults "keeping up in their field." And it simply makes for a better education. In allocating the resource of time, what higher priorities should there be than these?

Finally, private schools must rid themselves of their historically smug insularity and disdain for anything having to do with educational research and teacher training. Mistakenly equating colleges of education—historical descendants of normal schools—with educational research, they have assumed that the research science of education, only now beginning its second generation, has nothing to offer "liberal arts plus a little experience" school people. Reading educational research is a far different exercise from having to take a state-mandated certification course. The intellectual challenge, especially now, is daunting.

But in dealing with research, as always, educators must remind themselves and others of the richness of teaching and learning, to make real the findings of researchers so that students might learn more. As Noreen Garman says, in *School-Based Professional Development,*

> Teachers have continued to remind researchers that research language is impoverished because it neglects or fragments some of the most critical aspects of teaching, such as the *vitality* of the events, *faith* on the part of class members that something useful will happen, the *trust* and *caring* of participants, the presence of *humor* and *imagination* and the predisposition toward *success* instead of survival.

A crucial distinction

As we consider what and how to teach, at least two agendas are at work in a school curriculum, and we sometimes get them confused: the content agenda and the skills agenda. The content agenda refers to those facts, topics, ideas, and people to which we believe a student must be exposed in order to be educated. The skills agenda refers to those competences we consider essential to the student's future success, such as writing coherent sentences or computing basic arithmetic problems.

Sometimes a teacher's primary objective is to teach a particular skill, and she chooses to do so by way of some experience that would be independently valid as essential content. However, sometimes the content agenda and the skills agenda are confused, as in the case of a teacher who claims that his primary objective is to teach the ability to analyze poetry but who insists that this skill cannot be taught without extensive exposure to the sonnets of Shakespeare. Here a perfectly acceptable content objective is rationalized on the basis of a skill objective, which potentially undermines its credibility. Some teachers claim that they have only a skills agenda and that it doesn't really matter what the content is. The fact is that every teacher and every school makes value judgments about content. It is important to articulate the criteria.

TRY THIS . . .

Here are some fundamental questions to consider as you begin to broaden your horizons.

☞ What are the different theories of curriculum, and how do they inform, challenge, or affirm your definition of what is to be included under the rubric "curriculum"?

☞ What should be known about the curriculum recommendations of various professional groups such as the National Council of Teachers of Mathematics, the National Council of Teachers of English, the National Council for the Social Studies, the National Science Teachers Association, the International Reading Association, the National Art Education Association, the College Board, the National Association of Secondary School Principals, and the Association for Supervision and Curriculum Development?

☞ What vehicles are available for evaluating, monitoring, and assessing your curriculum? How might they be used to help either revise the current curriculum or plan for monitoring the projected curriculum?

☞ What are the current assumptions in your school about the nature of the learning process? Where and how are they articulated and used? How do those assumptions compare with current research?

☞ What assumptions about child development inform your curriculum? Are they consistent with current writing on the subject?

☞ What are the implications for your school of current research on learning styles and pedagogical thinking as related to race, gender, and class biases?

☞ How will you work toward a curriculum that is truly multicultural and that reflects the contributions of women and men?

☞ What do you identify as effective teaching in your school, and how does that square with current literature on the subject?

☞ How do you incorporate research on effective teaching in the design and implementation of the curriculum?

The content agenda has its roots in our notion of education as a process of initiation: "You must learn and value this because this is how you become one of us." A basic part of what it means to be educated is to have certain ideas and experiences firmly embedded in our mind—anything from the map of the world to the causes of World War I. The public outrage about surveys indicating that many college students can't place the Civil War in the correct half century, or can't distinguish between the basic tenets of Karl Marx and Thomas Jefferson, illustrates that as a society we have certain things we think people should know, quite apart from what they do with such knowledge. Learning those things becomes a criterion for being accepted into the "tribe," or at least the dominant tribe. But we know that the boundaries of the tribe, and therefore the definition of the essential content, have become very blurred.

The skills agenda has its roots in the notion that education is the source of empowerment and freedom: everything from learning to read so that you may be responsible for your own education to learning statistics so that you won't be fooled by clever canvassers and advertisers. Skills and competence make you powerful and independent. Not even the most radical behaviorist would claim that a skill can be learned in a vacuum, but the emphasis on skills over content changes the basis upon which curriculum is formulated and implemented. The emphasis is not on being accepted in a particular group but, rather, on being independent.

These two agendas coexist reasonably well, because both objectives—helping the student become a member of society and helping the student become free and powerful—are valid goals having a common motive. Problems arise when either rationale for instruction degenerates into a form of indoctrination. Deciding that all children should read a certain book, whether they are intellectually ready or not and whether that book validates their own heritage or does not, is an act of ideological indoctrination. Likewise, deciding that children should all learn a certain skill in order to improve the competitiveness of our national economy is not an act of empowerment but one of indoctrination, in this case based on utilitarianism. However, as long as the students' best interests remain our primary concern, we will have a trustworthy criterion for making decisions about what and how to teach.

Clarifying exercises

What follows is a series of clarifying exercises you can use either when curriculum review focuses on studying the internal workings of the school or when it makes an attempt to study the resources available from the outside. We encourage you to involve others in these exercises and to incorporate their findings into your review.

Dispositions

A definition: *A disposition is a propensity or tendency to think or behave a certain way, such as a disposition to be curious when confronting a new topic, a disposition to look for alternative solutions to a problem, or a disposition to express what is on one's mind.*

When we discuss curriculum in terms of student outcomes, we are often drawn to terms like "values" and "attitudes" to describe those objectives that are not specifically related to particular content and not readily measurable. Yet it is these intangibles that seem most important, both to us and to the parents and students who come to us. Early childhood specialist Lilian Katz uses the term "dispositions" to describe this kind of student outcome—a useful way to think about how our educational values and the actual instructional behaviors of the teacher come together.

Thinking about curriculum in light of the dispositions we would like students to develop provides another way of organizing the review process and thinking about what is essential and why.

What are the habits of heart and mind you wish to encourage in your students? Describe the dispositions that you hope the typical student in your school will possess at several "checkpoints." Next to each disposition, list those formal or planned experiences in the curriculum that promote the development of that disposition. Then discuss whether that connection is a real one, and whether the disposition deserves more attention. If it does, what will you do?

The Outline of Knowledge

In examining the content of a school's curriculum, it is useful to hold it up against an intentionally exhaustive outline of everything one might include. Such an outline is the basis for any encyclopedia. One version (the basic outline for the *Encyclopaedia Britannica III*) is available in an appendix to Mortimer Adler's book about the history of encyclopedic thinking, *A Guidebook to Learning*. This outline can be used as the basis for an audit or inventory.

Independent of the curriculum, faculty members can be asked to read through the outline, marking those items that they believe are absolutely essential to an education, those that are desirable or acceptable, and those that are best put off until later. A second review of the outline can look for those topics, from among the essentials and desirables, that provide the best opportunities for developing the skills and dispositions the teachers consider essential. The final review is made to determine the points of disagreement about what is essential (which can become the subject of important faculty dialogue), which essentials are currently absent from the curriculum, and which nonessentials are included and might be dropped. This is another angle on the "null curriculum" (see Chapter 7).

The point of this exercise is not to arrive at a new curriculum outline but to use the pre-established rubric of the encyclopedic outline to identify key points for debate and attention.

Essential Questions

Ask each teacher or department or grade level to think about curriculum in terms of the idea of "essential questions," as defined here by writer and consultant Grant Wiggins, in "Enabling Students To Be (Thoughtful) Workers," a white paper published by the Coalition of Essential Schools.

> Students are most engaged when the "work" is designed to be maximally thought-provoking and purposeful. That requires making intriguing questions and problems the heart of a curriculum. Organize courses not around "answers" but questions to which "content" represents answers. That requires having each teacher and the faculty as a whole know the questions their courses are designed to address, and making explicit to students that course work and materials suggest possible answers to those questions. Essential questions *(1) go to the heart of a discipline, (2) have no one obvious "right" answer, (3) are higher order involving analysis, synthesis and evaluative judgment*, and *(4) allow for personalized interest.*

What, for example, are the essential questions to which "French 2," "first grade," "physical education," and "glee club" are the answers? Push yourselves and one another on this.

Performances

Ask each teacher, department, or grade level to think about curriculum in terms of the idea of "performances," as defined by Grant Wiggins.

> Too many finals are designed for ease of grading, not as opportunities for being intellectually challenged and showing off one's competency, style and initiative in inquiry. Genuine mastery is a function of seeing and learning from one's mistakes in performance. We suggest that all teachers think of the course's goals in *functional* terms— an authentic final performance, a course-specific "performance" . . . more like the recital, play, final portfolio, college oral, or big games that are the culmination of and focal point for all prior study and practice. First design the "performances" that most embody or address the essential questions in an engaging, problem-solving way. Then design courses *backwards* around (leading to) those performances. Performances *(1) ask the student to engage in authentic inquiries, (2) require rehearsals, "scrimmages," and diagnosed practice, (3) require functional knowledge of the goal (the final performances should therefore be known as much in advance as is possible)*, and *(4) require knowledge of the criteria of "good" performance.*

Design final "performances" for a given course or grade and then consider the content, skills, and methods necessary to successful student performances.

The 25 Percent Problem

Assume you had 25 percent less time with your students than you currently have. What would you drop, and why?

Then assume you had 25 percent more time. What would you add or do more of, and why?

Compare the two lists. Is there anything on the "add" list that is more important or valuable than something on the "drop" list? If so, would it be possible simply to trade them off, with no change in your time with students? What are the common characteristics of the items on your drop list? On your add list? What do these lists tell you about your own educational values? Your own balance of agendas? How much agreement is there between your lists and those of your colleagues?

This is also a useful exercise to ask students, parents, board members, and graduates to do. Comparing lists from a variety of groups will generate valuable information and help guide your work.

"You Don't Work Here Any More"

This variant of "The 25 Percent Problem" is particularly useful and challenging for departments, forcing not only a hard look at what really counts but also suggesting possible approaches to interdisciplinary work.

Your school decides that your department (science, English, art) will cease to exist, but on your way out the door you may leave behind ten recommendations about how your department's mission and goals might be taken up by the departments that remain.

7.
The Hidden Curriculum and the Null Curriculum

Students in a History course are taught that Europe had an Enlightenment and a Renaissance. These terms—"Enlightenment" and "Renaissance"—focus attention on the activities, creations, and meanings important in particular ways for a particular group of men, who were then studied and written about by those trained to be professional historians. The Renaissance and the Enlightenment become, in students' minds, thing-events that contain, that were, an era's most significant and interesting reality. That the majority of the population—women and significant groups of men in Europe and in what have been called "the less developed countries"—experienced and understood these times in radically different ways is not considered worthy of much if any discussion.
    — Elizabeth Kamarck Minnich, *Transforming Knowledge*

Probably every teacher and administrator has had this experience: A former student comes back to visit, and in the course of the usual, sort of awkward "How's it going?" conversation, mentions something about you or something you did or didn't do that really made an impression on him . . . and *you can't remember it at all.* Or, if you do, you remember it as something unintentional or offhand. The conversation might make you feel wonderful—"I knew you really cared about me when you smiled at me after I failed that test"—or awful—"You know, you really played favorites in seventh grade"—or mystified—"Why didn't you teach us about slave culture?" However you feel, you have just encountered your own hidden or null curriculum.

Gail McCutcheon, in *The Curriculum*, offers the following definitions of the hidden and the null curriculum.

> The hidden curriculum is what students have an opportunity to learn through everyday goings-on under the auspices of schools, although teachers and other school people do not intend those learnings. . . . The null curriculum constitutes what students do not have an opportunity to learn under the auspices of the school.

In Elizabeth Minnich's passage about the Renaissance and the Enlightenment quoted above, the hidden curriculum is the activities of privileged white men alone being worthy of study; the null curriculum consists of the activities of women and other men that students do not have the opportunity to learn about.

The hidden curriculum

Virtually everything that happens in schools that is not subject to reflection and intention can be seen as part of the hidden curriculum. In his article "Innocence in Education," Benjamin Bloom argues that what is really important in schools is not what is formally taught but the pervasive and remarkably consistent lessons students learn from teachers' attitudes, regardless of the lesson plans, and from the environment of the school. This concept, that teaching has many unintended consequences, is the "hidden curriculum," the phrase usually carrying with it the same pejorative connotations as "hidden agenda." Understanding the hidden curriculum is crucial to any curriculum review, and any review that does not include an audit of the hidden curriculum is fundamentally flawed.

The hidden curriculum of any institution or system is made up of three elements, as defined by David Gordon in his article "The Concept of the Hidden Curriculum."

Outcomes: The nonacademic learnings promoted by schools, through the attitudes, dispositions, social skills, and dominant myths each school implicitly values

School environment: The physical and social environment in schools that contain hidden messages for students about social arrangements, relationships, and physical setting

Modes of influence: The unconscious and unintended teaching that occurs

The problem for schools is to determine where and how we teach our hidden curriculum and then to evaluate it. It is important to understand that just because something is unintentional and "hidden" does not necessarily mean that it is negative. But you can't evaluate the hidden curriculum if you can't identify it. Identifying negative aspects of the hidden curriculum makes it possible to change them; identifying positive aspects makes it possible to capitalize on them.

Here are some examples of unintended, "hidden" messages in schools.

- Grading on a fixed curve produces pleasing symmetry but teaches that learning is about competition and that success for one is tied to failure for another.

- Student handbooks with endless lists of byzantine rules create, perhaps, a sense of order and fair play but also imply a pessimistic view of human nature and behavior and suggest that social relationships are nothing more than an intricate game—a game that students may be very willing to play.

53

TRY THIS . . .

☞ List ten important academic or curricular policies ("Reading groups are defined by ability," "Every course will have a final exam") and try to define the implicit, unintended messages of each policy.

☞ Visit, as a team, your school on a weekend or during a vacation, when no one is around. Try to include someone from outside the school. Think of yourselves as archaeologists and anthropologists charged with describing the school's culture and mythology based *exclusively* on the artifacts you see.

☞ Take your team and go off for a day; the leaving is crucial. Take with you a year's worth of official school publications: yearbook, newsletter, course descriptions, handbooks, calendar of events, fund-raising letters, admission brochures, school videos—anything that the school has created to communicate with its constituents. What are the explicit and implicit messages? What are the images that dominate? What do those images really mean? What unintended teaching happens through these publications?

☞ What are the subtle behaviors that get punished or rewarded at your school? What is the cumulative effect of this system?

☞ Shadow a student for a day, focusing only on the implicit messages the school transmits.

☞ Gather a group of students or teachers or parents and ask them to tell you what the school really believes is important and how they know it.

☞ Look at your rituals. What are you celebrating?

• Talking about the "girls' soccer team," but just saying "soccer team" when we mean the boys' team, suggests that boys are the norm, girls the exception.

• "It could be argued that the purpose of mathematics curriculum is not only to enable pupils to learn mathematics but also to allow some to understand that they cannot learn mathematics and acquire a suitable respect for those who can." — John Eggleston, *The Sociology of the School Curriculum*

This is not to argue that everyone should do away with grading curves, student handbooks, and the traditional mathematics curriculum. But people in schools need to understand what they are implicitly teaching and decide whether that is in fact what they wish to convey.

Auditing the hidden curriculum can be done at virtually every level: in a class, a department, a division, or the whole school. The same awareness can help individuals understand how and what they communicate.

The null curriculum

"Null curriculum," a newer concept, is equally important for a curriculum review. Elliot Eisner, in *The Educational Imagination*, defines it as "that which we choose not to teach" and posits three categories of the null curriculum.

Subject matter. Sometimes we choose not to teach an entire field: economics, law, psychology and anthropology, to choose a few. Or a subfield: in history, we choose not to teach the history of science. Or a given concept of a subject matter: some schools in their biology classes don't teach evolution. Or even the facts in a subject: we might teach the New Deal without mentioning that it failed to solve the problem of unemployment. Some of these choices are conscious, others simply result from what happens to be included in the textbooks we select.

Intellectual processes. Few schools teach visual, auditory, metaphoric, and synesthetic modes of thought, which are nonverbal and alogical.

Affect. As compared to the hidden curriculum, in which we are not *aware* of what we are doing, in this aspect of the null curriculum we *choose* not to teach or honor certain values, attitudes, and emotions.

What are the practical implications of this concept of null curriculum for a curriculum review?

We can sit around and discuss the effects of not exposing women to auto mechanics or men to the culinary arts. But we can also (1) do a thorough and deliberate review of the alternatives, (2) re-examine goals and selection criteria in light of content, and (3) sharpen the focus of implementation. This is not to suggest that any school can or should try to do everything, but rather that every school should have clear, consistent reasons for its particular null curriculum.

TRY THIS . . .

☞ Ask each department, division, or grade level to make a presenta-tion about the significant content and skills it *does* not teach and the sound pedagogical methods they have *chosen* not to use and the reasons behind those decisions. An added benefit of this exercise is increased ability to articulate these decisions to others who might ask.

☞ Ask your students, their parents, and your graduates what it was that you didn't teach. Do they understand why you didn't?

☞ Examine a random sample of textbooks and see what is missing.

☞ Examine a random sample of tests and exams. What skills and knowledge are not tested?

☞ Whose voice, history, or culture is missing from your curriculum?

☞ What is missing from the school's public spaces?

☞ What is the null curriculum of the school's library?

☞ As a thought experiment, ask people to define what it is you are doing that should be moved into the null curriculum and why.

For example, in a small school the teacher of a music course chooses individual vocal lessons over a small chorus because individual lessons make for better practicing musicians. But should the goal of the course be to make the students practicing musicians? The null curriculum teaches educators to start with the goals of their work and have content and methods flow from those goals. Deciding what to not teach should be a reflective exercise, not just an accident.

Understanding these two curricula, the hidden and the null, is an essential step in any curriculum review. If the review is limited to only considering permutations of what is already explicitly being done, important opportunities for inquiry and transformation are lost.

DON'T FORGET!

In thinking about implementation, the most important action with these two other curricula is the act of recognition: the hidden curriculum is revealed, the null curriculum is consciously defined. Working from this recognition, goals can be established and implemented, sometimes immediately. If you don't like what you find, change it.

8.
Sample Process
for Curriculum
Review

The unhappy person is one who is possessed by some idea which he cannot convert into action. — Goethe

Reflection, research, and discussion are crucial to curriculum review, but they must be converted to action through a coherent process that gathers momentum and leads to substantive change. There are three basic levels of curriculum review: whole school, small group, and individual teacher. While each review has special circumstances and requirements, the same basic process applies in each case. This chapter walks through that basic process, referring both to the narrative chapters and to the detailed questions in Chapter 10. This chapter, by design, repeats and reinforces many of the points made elsewhere.

Curriculum reviews by small groups and individual teachers are probably the most familiar and also the least intimidating to schools: for example, the lower or elementary school works on reading, the science department reorders upper or high school sequence, or the middle school art teacher develops a new unit on color. These efforts often overlap. Sometimes an individual teacher may identify a problem with her course and set out to solve it, but when the problem seems to extend beyond a single classroom a small group forms to address it more broadly.

This kind of review is most often seen as clearly delimited, falling neatly within one or more of the myriad "boxes" we create within our schools. Sometimes people will even go to some length to reassure those around them—in those other "boxes"—that what they are doing won't affect anyone else (as if it couldn't). Typically these efforts are reactive; like most institutions, schools go with the "If it ain't broke, don't fix it" philosophy (of course, that "it" is not obviously broken does not necessarily mean that "it" is worthwhile). And often we do in fact fix what seems to be broken, or we shunt the pressure to another part of the school and wait to see what happens.

Schools experience the whole-school level of curriculum review much less frequently. For most, this happens every seven or ten years when they prepare the self-study that forms part of the school's accreditation renewal. Many accreditation processes include excellent material to guide a school's "audit" of its programs. Even so, because of the many other demands of the accreditation process, and because these processes by their very nature focus on describing the status quo, schools seem hard put to use the occasion to do more than determine what they are presently doing.

Schools will always have to cope with particular problems, and regular accreditation procedures are useful and necessary, but we encourage them to consider a more proactive approach, to take the time now to think about what they are doing and why they are doing it. We believe that this is exciting and important work that, when carried out regularly, will mean fewer "fires" to put out, a richer and more productive self-study at accreditation time, and better teaching and learning.

The process we recommend has six stages.

- Seeing the need

- Getting started

- Self-examination: determining what you have

- Research: broadening horizons

- Goal setting: determining what you want

- Implementation and evaluation: making things happen

It is important to remember that this is not a ruggedly linear process with neatly encapsulated stages. Your process will work best if you allow for revising, rethinking, and circling back—always keeping your goals in sight. The following descriptions of each stage focus on group review examples; an individual teacher would move through the same stages. Chapter 10, "Questions for Curriculum Review," offers questions to use during each stage.

Seeing the need

While obvious, it is important to state that the first step in the process is recognizing the need for review and change. Curriculum review is hard work, and even if you believe that it should happen regularly you have to balance that belief against all of the other demands you face.

How, then, does a school or a group or an individual teacher know when it is time to take a thoughtful look at curriculum? Here are some indications that curriculum review should receive high priority.

- You are thinking of adding a division or series of new grades.

- Some significant/traumatic/destabilizing event or series of events has led you to question your program.

- A major shift in the racial/cultural/socioeconomic background of your community, student body, or preferred admission pool has taken place.

- Your school is due to merge with another school or schools.

- A significant shift in enrollment patterns makes it necessary for your private school to enlarge, become smaller, or attract new types of students, such as those with learning differences, underachievers, postgraduates, or foreign students.

- Your curriculum needs to honor equally the voices, contributions, and history of men and women.

- Your curriculum needs to honor the voices, contributions, and history of a variety of peoples and cultures, especially people of color.

- Your school has had exceptionally heavy faculty turnover; course and curriculum content can change rapidly and haphazardly when faculty turnover is heavy.

- Your school has exceptionally light faculty turnover; low turnover reinforces the power of the status quo.

- Your school has not undertaken such a review in a long time.

- Your school has new leadership.

- The visiting committee of your accrediting body has identified problem areas in your curriculum.

- Your curriculum seems to be at odds with credible new research findings or new recommendations or standards from credible organizations.

- Changes in educational technology suggest new possibilities.

- You want to encourage staff collaboration and growth.

- Concerns expressed about your program by students, parents, or graduates are becoming more numerous or seem to be coalescing into specific patterns.

- You need to respond to parents' demands for new programs and have to be able to justify your response.

- The schools with which you compete—public and private—are making significant curricular changes that may make them more attractive.

- The requirements or expectations of the next level of education to which your students are headed have changed.

- The requirements or expectations of the prior level of education from which your students come have changed.

- What worked last year or three years ago or ten years ago doesn't seem to work any more.

- It sounds like fun or it does not sound like fun.

Once you have recognized the need for curriculum review, the process itself begins.

Getting started

The person or persons who recognized the need for curriculum review must now share that belief widely and convincingly, bringing with them those who by virtue of their formal or informal authority, their influence, their expertise, or their title will be crucial to a good start. All of these people may not actually be part of the group that does the review, but their initial and ongoing support is pivotal. As you get started, think about the last successful change at the school and the last unsuccessful change and factor the lessons learned into your planning. Consider, too, how your school's culture will or may shape the review process (see Chapter 3, "School Culture").

Except when a teacher begins a review alone, the first task of a review is to form a group. Those responsible for creating the group must choose wisely from among all the appropriate constituencies (see Chapter 1, "Involving Others"). In making these choices, look for people who have a certain amount of expertise in curriculum development and others who have political influence and understanding; choose those who will make the time in their lives for the work, those willing to read and research, and those who are devoted to the school and its mission and able to be both dispassionate and passionate (see Chapter 10, "Questions for Curriculum Review").

A balance of temperaments, experience, biases, and strengths must be struck, but within this healthy diversity there should be a clear commitment to good group process. Those who do not work as well as others in a group might be asked to take on discrete tasks later on in the process. (See Chapter 1, "Involving Others," and Chapter 2, "Teaching and Leading," for a full discussion of the roles each group plays.)

Those responsible for forming the group must also decide how to make the necessary time and resources available to planners. A whole-school review may take as long as an academic year, if not longer. Chunks of concentrated time are needed for the initial strategizing and advance planning; for committee members to get to know one another and to reach some common understanding of the group's charge, the school's goals, mission, and values; for research into the substantive pieces of the project; and for reaching agreement or consensus on curriculum goals and plans for implementing them. (See Chapter 2, "Teaching and Leading," and Chapter 5, "Time and Schedule.")

In addition to time and resources, the group must start with a clear assignment and at least a tentative timeline: "Study the lower school science sequence and make recommendations before spring vacation." The group itself may have to redefine its task and timeline as work progresses: "We have also to look at the math sequence, and that will take six weeks more." Clarify also how, when, and to whom the group reports and to whom it is immediately and ultimately accountable: "The group will report every two weeks to the lower school head and will consult with the head of school before defining specific goals."

Watch out for these group traps . . .

☞ *The good group circular reasoning trap.* "We're a good group, so everything we do is good; and since everything we do is good, we're a good group." Good groups can make bad decisions (and vice versa).

☞ *The in group–out group trap.* This trap is best sprung or avoided by careful selection of members and good communication with other constituencies.

☞ *The "let's be nice" trap.* When being nice is valued above all else, it is hard to accomplish anything worthwhile.

☞ *The consensus at any cost trap.* Moving too quickly to consensus *for its own sake* can stifle inspiration and productive debate.

☞ *The "we've already decided that" trap.* Revisiting previous decisions has to be acceptable, within reason.

Self-examination: determining what you have

With its assignment in hand, the group then engages in a series of tasks based on the premise that if you don't know exactly what you have in your present curriculum, you cannot decide what you want to keep and what you want to change. The tasks may be separate and simultaneous—one group working on language arts, another examining math and science, for example—and at this point should heavily involve others and always address the question of keeping people informed of the committee's work. Some people might study the school's mission, while others describe present content and methods. The results of these inquiries are brought back to the review group for assimilation. The goal is a kind of snapshot or portrait of what is going on in the relevant areas of the school's program.

This may seem quite straightforward; many schools, after all, have detailed course descriptions and scope and sequence charts that will save time here. But organized auditing and description of *teaching methods* is, in fact, relatively unusual in many schools. It is easy to succumb to the temptation not only to separate content from method but also to believe that that separation is in fact legitimate. So, as you track curriculum content, track the ways in which that material is taught.

Thinking about the culture of the school should help the group to begin to define the best ways to accomplish its task and to understand the barriers that must be overcome (see Chapter 3, "School Culture," and Chapter 4, "Overcoming Barriers"). Implementation, in a sense, actually begins here, with questions about what facilitates and what stands in the way of getting things done. Sometimes planners do need to liberate themselves from thinking about implementation, but to lose sight of it for too long, even early on, is to court disaster. Remembering that ideas must be converted into actions, the group maintains the useful tension between planning and implementation.

By the end of this stage, the group has compiled and fully assimilated an accurate portrait of the school's (or division's or department's) curriculum and pedagogy. This portrait has great value in and of itself and should be shared with the entire faculty; it can also be used for communicating about the school's program with different constituencies within the school community.

Finally, the group should not move out of this stage without establishing a clear plan for communicating its work to others along the way.

Research: broadening horizons

The next step for the group is to move beyond the school and the status quo and to consider other possibilities, on the premise that it is hard to decide what you want if you don't know what the choices are (see Chapter 6, "Broadening Horizons").

At this point, a useful first step is for the group to articulate its assumptions about curriculum (see the Introduction for the assumptions that guide this book) and to adopt the definition of curriculum that seems most useful. Developing and embracing a common set of beliefs and a common language are crucial to the ultimate coherence of curricular goals (see Chapter 10, "Questions for Curriculum Review").

From this common ground, the group moves on to some consideration of the future (see Chapter 10), to thought experiments about ideal student outcomes, and to a review of the relevant theory and research (see "Resources"). We encourage you to explore material in curriculum theory, learning theory, child development, and pedagogy. The resources are, of course, too numerous for any group to command completely, but a broad scan is necessary. The group should end with a good sense of what is "out there" and be prepared to base its goals on this external knowledge as well as on an understanding of the school and its needs.

At this point or even sooner, the group might engage in some of the clarifying exercises presented in Chapter 6, "Broadening Horizons," and invite other groups to do the same. Parents, for example, could be asked to define ideal student outcomes or dispositions, a department could work to devise essential questions or performances, and a division might tackle the 25 percent problem. Involving others helps the group think broadly and is a way of smoothing the road to acceptance and implementation.

Finally, the group must seek ways to share the results of its explorations and findings with others, thus providing information, identifying problems, and building support.

Goal setting: determining what you want

From the knowledge of what is going on inside your school, what resources are available outside, and the possibilities for change, broad curricular goals begin to emerge, perhaps many of them. The actual scope of the various goals will be somewhat determined by the original assignment, but the group may well have decided that the original task was too narrow or too broad. We urge you to be open always to new ideas and paths; what started out as an effort to revise the lower school science sequence may end up as a plan also to integrate science more fully into the rest of the curriculum.

The group lists curricular goals in order of priority, gives the rationale for each goal, and indicates, in broad strokes, further implementation steps and an approximate timetable for completion.

> Given the school's commitment to diversity, the increasing size of the city's Latino community, and the school's Latino enrollment, the middle school language arts and social studies curriculum will include significant units on the history and culture of Mexico and Latin America. The first of these units will be developed this summer and put into place and evaluated by the end of the next school year.

Finally, when the goals are defined, draw up specific suggestions as to how and when the goals are going to be implemented and evaluated, recognizing that those charged with implementation and evaluation must be able to incorporate their own ideas and strategies into the task. The crucial questions are "What will we do?" and "How will we know if it is working?"

This brings the planning process to its conclusion, making way for implementation, which has been shadowing planning, to take over and bring about change.

Implementation and evaluation: making things happen

Implementation often gets shortchanged; many a consultant's study or new curriculum sits forlornly on the shelf because people ran out of energy or resources or support or will or nerve. Or because the reality of change was too intimidating for people who had not been well prepared for it.

In virtually every chapter we try to combat the tendency to talk and talk and never act. Planning is, of course, a form of action, but we all know how much easier it is to talk about curriculum change than it is to convince people to change the way they think about the school and their roles in it. In Chapter 10 are questions to help guide you through implementation. Don't forget that implementation must include monitoring and evaluation checkpoints so that the success of each effort may be tested and new strategies be developed as needed. The curriculum is a hypothesis that must constantly be tested.

We believe that this review process produces tangible benefits for the school even before formal implementation begins and that those benefits will help sustain the energy and commitment needed for implementing curricular goals. Ideally, the staff and the school leadership have been well informed of the group's work and timetable and have begun, in some small ways at least, to gear up for implementation. Using the diversity goal mentioned above, for example, the head may have already made some funds available to support summer curriculum development; the middle school head may have begun to figure out a way to include a common planning period for language arts and social studies teachers in next year's schedule; and individual teachers may have already begun reading and conferring with colleagues in other schools.

Look back over the previous chapters and pick out the sections headed "Don't Forget!" where we stress that implementation can take place without goals having been completely formulated. We believe that real, beneficial action can occur during the process itself.

The curriculum review committee can—and must—model good group process to the community. Auditing what is going on inside a school can by itself create change and improvement as people see things that can be "fixed" right away, whether they relate to the review committee's charge or not. Studying the school culture, observing the pedagogy, reflecting on the barriers to change, and informing the community about relevant research— these important parts of the planning process must be converted as soon as possible into action to serve the community, no matter what the final goals are.

Good process is both a means to an end and an end in itself. When you get to your formal, specific curricular goals, you will already be well on the way to meeting them.

9.
Coherence, Complexity, and Interdependence

Good schools are . . . preoccupied with the rationale, coherence, and integrity of their curriculum.
— Sara Lawrence Lightfoot, *The Good High School*

In *The Youngest Science* Lewis Thomas describes a puzzling phenomenon he encountered in medical school during an experiment injecting rabbits with papain, a protein-splitting enzyme. For several days after the injections, the rabbits' ears became limp and floppy, yet with microscopes Thomas and his fellow students could detect no abnormality of the cells in the rabbits' ears. Eventually, they discovered that, while the injections had no effect on the cells, the papain virtually dissolved the matrix surrounding the cells. Without the supporting matrix, the rabbits' ears could not retain their stiffness: the normal function of rabbits' ears was a complex interdependence of cells and matrix.

Ideally, a good school displays the same kind of complex interdependence. There are individual cells—students and teachers and so on—each at work side by side. A student seeks to learn, to take a few bruises, and grow; a teacher, to enlighten and get the grades in on time; a school head, to lead and survive the next board meeting; a parent, to endure until the child journeys out; and a board member, to set policy, direct certain telephone calls to the school head, and raise funds.

The matrix of a good school is what unites these people. It is often unspoken and unseen, even under a microscope. It is the "feel" of the school—a way of being and of doing business that unites the student awaiting word from college with the teacher struggling to find enough resources for fourth grade social studies, as well as the head waiting to speak with a major donor, and the parent at a party answering questions about the school.

A good curriculum—once again, ideally—is also a complex interdependence of cells and matrix. What marvelous cells there can be: the English–history unit in seventh grade; the first grade reading, writing, drawing, and singing about dinosaurs; the collaborative bill-writing project in government class; community service with the cerebral palsy center; the state championship basketball game. The matrix of a good curriculum joins together what happens in and out of the classroom, builds all aspects of the child—intellectual, moral, and physical—and supports the age-old quest of the child becoming an adult.

A curriculum review process must understand this unique nature of schools and curriculum—that, no matter how microscopic the examination of one cell, that cell, in order to function, depends upon the matrix of the school. This is not to say that a curriculum process must examine the whole school or nothing at all. But if a curriculum review focuses on writing across the curriculum in the middle school, for example, it cannot assume that revising the approach to writing in grades 6-8 will not reverberate through all the grades.

A curriculum review might well model itself after this interdependence of the parts and the whole. The parts are multiple: a steering committee of engaged people, teachers auditing what is taught and how, time and money to do the work, expert advice, and so on. The whole is a community-wide assent to self-examination, to an ongoing and essential process not to be feared but welcomed. Self-examination strengthens the matrix of the curriculum, that sense of the child becoming an adult. And, if the curriculum review is free of destructive injections of cynicism, laziness, exclusivity, and world weariness, then surely it strengthens the matrix of the school.

And yet . . . a curriculum review, no matter how much it presses toward the goal of coherence, must also recognize that schools, like all social groups, are complex, at times terribly incoherent, and imperfect. Drawing her own portraits of schools, in *The Good High School*, Sarah Lawrence Lightfoot writes,

> The assumption is that no school will ever achieve perfection. It is inconceivable that any institution would ever establish an equilibrium that satisfied all of its inhabitants, where values closely matched behaviors, where there was no tension between tradition and change. Even the most impressive schools show striking moments of vulnerability, inconsistency, and awkwardness. It is not the absence of weakness that marks a good school, but how a school attends to the weakness.

Curriculum review must, then, steer the difficult course between a hoped-for coherence as philosophically neat as Plato's republic and the hard-edged truth that no one ever promised that life or school was neat.

10.
Questions for
Curriculum Review

This chapter provides an outline and specific questions to assist in the process of curriculum review. In no way do we consider the questions to be exhaustive. We do hope they encourage you to address important issues and to discuss the best way to organize the process. We also hope they help you generate a new set of questions more specific to your school and to the scope of your review.

The questions are organized to follow the process steps described in Chapter 8. The same questions can be used by groups or by an individual. The fundamental approach is always the same and the steps are as follows.

- Seeing the need

- Getting started

- Self-examination: determining what you have

- Research: broadening horizons

Questions

- Goal setting: determining what you want

- Implementation and evaluation: making things happen

Seeing the need

1. For whom is curriculum review a priority? For whom is it not a priority?

2. Are the leaders of the school interested in curriculum review and willing to allocate energy, time, commitment, money, and people to the task?

3. Do one or more of the following circumstances apply to your school?

- You are thinking of adding a division or series of new grades.

- Some significant/traumatic/destabilizing event or series of events has led you to question your program.

- A major shift in the racial/cultural/socioeconomic background of your community, student body, or preferred admission pool has taken place.

- Your school is due to merge with another school or schools.

- A significant shift in enrollment patterns makes it necessary for your private school to enlarge, become smaller, or attract new types of students, such as those with learning differences, underachievers, postgraduates, or foreign students.

- Your curriculum needs to honor equally the voices, contributions, and history of men and women.

- Your curriculum needs to honor the voices, contributions, and history of a variety of peoples and cultures, especially people of color.

- Your school has had exceptionally heavy faculty turnover; course and curriculum content can change rapidly and haphazardly when faculty turnover is heavy.

- Your school has exceptionally light faculty turnover; low turnover reinforces the power of the status quo.

- Your school has not undertaken such a review in a long time.

- Your school has new leadership.

- The visiting committee of your accrediting body has identified problem areas in your curriculum.

- Your curriculum seems to be at odds with credible new research findings or new recommendations or standards from credible organizations.

- Changes in educational technology suggest new possibilities.

- You want to encourage staff collaboration and growth.

- Concerns expressed about your program by students, parents, or graduates are becoming more numerous or seem to be coalescing.

- You need to respond to parents' demands for new programs and have to be able to justify your response.

- The schools with which you compete—public and private— are making significant curricular changes that may make them more attractive.

- The requirements or expectations of the next level of education to which your students are headed have changed.

- The requirements or expectations of the prior level of education from which your students come have changed.

Questions

- What worked last year or three years ago or ten years ago doesn't seem to work any more.

- It sounds like fun or it does not sound like fun.

Getting started

Basic factors

1. Is the school head in a position of strength?

2. What factions have built up around parts of the curriculum?

3. What external agendas will surface when curriculum review begins?

4. Can you start right off with a curriculum review, or will you need to make structural or cultural changes first?

5. How will you decide if the process would be enhanced by using a consultant?

6. How will you gather the support and momentum you need to get started and see the review through to completion?

7. What can you learn from the last successful committee at the school? What can you learn from the last unsuccessful committee?

8. What can you learn from the last major change in the school, successful or unsuccessful?

9. Who will be the key players in the politics of change in your school, whether they are actively involved or not? Where are the formal and informal vetoes?

10. Who needs to know what you are considering?

| Forming the group |

1. Who will select the review group? On what basis?

2. How inclusive can the group be (all divisions and departments, board members, administrators, faculty members, parents, graduates, students, outside experts)?

3. What will the group's characteristics be (size, expertise, political clout, availability and willingness to commit to the project, ability to be dispassionate and passionate, style of interaction)?

4. What will the scope of the review be? Should it include the school's mission, explicit curriculums and co-curriculum, implicit or "hidden" curriculum, educational policies and practices, the "null" curriculum?

5. How long should the review take? How will you decide the timetable?

6. What resources will be needed to support the group (secretarial help, budget for consultant, retreat facilities, supplies, books, duplication of reading materials)?

7. What kind of preparation should members of the group have?

8. What will be the specific charge of the group? Who will define this?

9. What message do you want to send through the composition of the group?

10. How will you avoid the in group–out group trap?

11. What strengths and weaknesses, what "baggage," will each group member bring?

12. Who will lead and facilitate the group? How will leaders be chosen?

13. If needed, how will you provide release time for the group?

14. How can you schedule meetings to maximize effectiveness?

15. To whom, how often, and in what manner will the group report?

16. To whom is the group ultimately accountable?

17. Who must be kept aware of the group's work?

18. Will there be adjunct meetings with constituent groups, such as faculty, students, and parents, to assure their contribution to and support for the project?

Self-examination: determining what you have

Clarifying assumptions

Here are the basic assumptions about curriculum that guided the discussions of the NAIS Academic Services Committee.

- Curriculum is best defined as all the experiences children have under the guidance of teachers and/or school. This view considers almost anything in school, even outside school (so long as it is planned).

- The primary goal of any curriculum review is to provide students with a better education.

- Teachers take the central role in transforming and implementing curriculum.

- Curriculum review is challenging and sometimes painful.

- Planning and implementation of curriculum must be conscious, deliberate, and open.

- Curriculum content and pedagogy are inextricably linked. Curriculum planning must examine both.

- Curriculum and curriculum planning are inherently political and never value-free. Making the underlying values of curriculum explicit is crucial. We believe, for example, that curriculum and pedagogy should specifically address and seek to correct race, ethnic, gender, and class bias.

- Establishing the goals and values of a school's curriculum should include representatives of the school's major constituencies

1. What reactions do you have to this list? How do these assumptions make you feel—angry? affirmed? challenged?

2. Which assumptions do you immediately identify as being consistent with your own beliefs?

3. Would you express any of the assumptions differently? How?

4. Would others in your school agree with these assumptions?

5. Are your school's assumptions stated somewhere? In what form?

6. Which assumptions do not make sense or seem ambivalent?

7. Which assumptions do you reject? Why?

8. What is missing? What do you need to add or subtract to end up with assumptions that reflect your beliefs? Create your own list.

9. If you published your assumptions tomorrow, how would people react? Would they be surprised? Who would be angry? Who would feel threatened? Who would embrace them? Who would feel affirmed?

10. With whom could you share these assumptions?

11. What have you learned from doing this? How could it help the curriculum review process?

Defining curriculum

Using a process similar to the one you used above in defining your assumptions, you may find it useful to articulate for yourself and others your own working definition of curriculum.

1. What things come to mind when you think of curriculum?

2. Can you exclude some things from your list? Which ones? Why?

3. How is curriculum defined by those who write about it?

4. How does your school generally define curriculum?

- What school documents provide this definition? If none do, what might that mean?
- Are there differences of definition among the various school constituencies? What are the most critical differences?
- How might these differences influence your project?
- What values are implicit in these definitions?

5. Define your school's hidden curriculum—those things that, while unintentional, convey certain attitudes, values, and expectations. How might this hidden curriculum facilitate or block your project? What can you do about it?

6. Define your school's "null curriculum"—those things that the school has chosen not to teach. What are the implications of this null curriculum for your project?

7. How has your definition of curriculum changed?

8. How should the school's definition of curriculum change?

| *School mission, educational goals, and social justice values* |

1. Gather all the formal, written statements published by the school that address curriculum policy, models of the graduate as an "educated citizen," college and career attitudes, learning and teaching, and social justice (assumptions about the school's mission in relation to the values of parents, students, teachers, and the community). What exactly do all these documents say, and what does it mean?

2. What implicit assumptions operate in the school's mission, educational goals, and social values?

3. If there are apparent contradictions between the school's mission and your project, how might you resolve them? With whom must you consult?

4. To what degree does the school seek, welcome, and support diversity in terms of

—people?

—curriculum?

—policy and procedures?

—culture and climate?

5. How will these policies, practices, and attitudes inform your work?

6. Given the information you have gathered, what are its implications for curriculum planning?

Profile of community, school, students, parents, and faculty
---

1. How would you describe the community in which your school exists in terms of

—the region?

—the culture of the community?

—special features, such as tourism and high tech industry?

2. What community resources are available to the school and to you?

3. What is your school's major competition?

4. Who attends your school and why?

5. How would you describe the typical student or graduate of your school in terms of

—academic ability?

—next school or college?

—special talents or interests?

—values?

6. Why do students leave your school? What are the characteristics of those who leave?

7. How would you describe the parent body in terms of

—income and professional level?

—ethnic, racial, and class mix?

—attitudes and values?

8. Who teaches in your school? What are the special qualities of the faculty? What qualities are most valued by the school?

Research: broadening horizons

Personal experience

Think back to your own school experience, focusing on the years matching the grade levels in your present school. Try to recall an event or interaction that had a lasting effect on you. Was it the result of planned, deliberate activity on the part of a teacher or the school as a whole? If not, try to think of an experience that was and describe it in writing and sharing it with the group. What have you learned?

The ideal student

1. Describe the ideal student at your school at various grade levels. Be concrete and focus on those strengths, skills, and values that you feel are the result of, or at least supported and nurtured by, the school experience. Then ask

- What does this student know?
- What can this student do?
- What does this student care about?

2. What school experiences probably support the development of such a student, and which ones are probably irrelevant to this development?

Clarifying exercises

In addition to the suggestions offered here, consider the clarifying exercises given in Chapter 6, "Broadening Horizons." Any exercise that helps you shake off old ways of thinking is all to the good; thought experiments are just that.

Questions

Thinking about the future

Thinking about the future may be useful to you as you begin to plan. You will have to decide which future (near or far) to consider and how wide or narrow the scope (global, national, your school, or just one classroom) will be. The following questions may help as you create your vision of the future as it relates to your project.

1. What are the salient features of life in that future? How will these features affect your school, its students, and your curriculum?

2. What are your greatest hopes and worst fears for this future?

3. What will the relevant demography (national or local) be? What effect will this have on your curriculum?

4. What kinds of students and families will you be working with?

5. What will the values of these people be?

6. What is the likely profile of your colleagues in this future?

7. What facilities, materials, and technologies will be available? What effect will they have on your curriculum?

8. How will new educational technology affect teaching and learning? Describe in writing the future (say, 2010) as you see it.

9. How will the school be funded?

10. What political and legal factors are likely to affect the school?

11. What global issues will affect the curriculum in the next ten years —the economic importance of the Pacific rim, the growing Spanish-speaking population in the U.S., distrust of government and public officials, declining voter turnout, declining church and synagogue attendance?

12. What state and local issues will affect the curriculum in the next ten years? How could the school best respond to these issues—by considering a required course in ethics and citizenship, adding Japanese as a modern language offering, developing a stress management and mental health awareness program for students?

13. How can these assumptions about the future best be confirmed or discredited—through state, local, corporate, and regional projections? educational research? books and articles on future trends?

Present curriculum and pedagogy

1. Collect material you already have about the curriculum you wish to review (course outlines or descriptions, scope and sequence studies, the last accreditation report, other material). If this material does not presently exist in a useful form, how can you gather it?

2. What other "auditing" tools might be helpful to you?

3. Does the material you gather correspond to your definition of curriculum?

4. How can the group, or the individual, best assimilate the present state of the curriculum in order to think constructively about change?

5. What material is available in the school describing the present state of pedagogy in the school? How can you find out how the curriculum is taught?

6. What statements does the school make about the teaching methods it endorses? To what extent are those methods actually used? How were those methods chosen?

7. What can you learn about methods from the school's system of evaluation and professional development?

8. What repertory of methods is available to teachers? How do they balance those methods within a given day or class and throughout the year?

9. What methods do you use to encourage critical thinking? imaginative thinking?

10. How do you balance lecture, discovery, large groups, and small groups?

11. How does the school support individual learning? cooperative learning?

12. How do present methods allow for different learning styles?

13. How are methods evaluated for effectiveness?

14. How are methods discussed, reviewed, affirmed, or changed?

15. What have you learned from this consideration of present methods?

Consulting relevant research

1. What are the major schools of curriculum theory? What are the explicit and implicit agendas of writers on curriculum, and how does that influence your thinking? How would you categorize your school's present curriculum? Why? How does this affect your project?

2. What research on curriculum should be consulted, given your charge and the scope of your review?

3. What do you need to know about the curriculum theories, approaches, and recommendations of professional groups such as the National Council of Teachers of Mathematics, the National Association for the Education of Young Children, the National Art Education Association, and the Association for Supervision and Curriculum Development? (See "Resources" for the names and addresses of these and other organizations.)

- Which of their theories, approaches, and recommendations might you use for your project?
- Which of their theories, approaches, or recommendations do you specifically reject? on what grounds? Will you need to make a "case" for rejection to someone at some point?

4. What tools are available for evaluating, monitoring, and assessing your curriculum?

5. What are the current assumptions, implicit and explicit, about the nature of the learning process in your school? How do those assumptions compare with current research?

6. What are your current assumptions about learning styles?

7. What are the implications of current research on learning styles and pedagogical thinking as they relate to gender, race, and class biases?

8. What do you identify as effective teaching in your school?

9. How will you incorporate research on effective teaching into the design of a better curriculum?

10. What assumptions, implicit and explicit, about child development exist in your school? How do those assumptions compare with the current state of research?

11. How will you ensure that your project is developmentally appropriate?

Goal setting: determining what you want

Involving others

1. How can you effectively share the information you have gathered with others?

2. How can others best be involved in processing the information you gather?

3. What personal response is needed from others—more information? personal experiences? immediate reactions? clarifying questions?

4. What educational outcomes—skills, knowledge—do you anticipate for students? How can you involve them at this juncture?

5. Have you involved parents or the broader community yet? If not, when will you?

Emerging goals, plans, desired outcomes

1. What does all of your work suggest as far as goals for the development of curriculum in the school are concerned?

2. What current school practices do you wish to reaffirm? What new practices do you wish to encourage?

3. Do a first list of goals, plans, and desired outcomes, considering the following questions for each.

- What is the rationale behind each curricular goal the committee has identified?
- How does each goal reflect the educational values of the school?
- How does each goal relate to your underlying assumptions about curriculum?

- How does each goal relate to accepted curriculum theory?

- How does the goal reflect current research in pedagogy, especially as it relates to learning styles and developmental needs?

- What outcomes do you anticipate for students?

- How will you disseminate the goals? Who is the primary audience? the secondary audience?

- What will you need to do to prepare people for the goals?

- Are you willing to have others add or subtract goals? If so, what will be the process for making that happen?

- How can you engage others in planning possible implementation steps?

- What will the indicators of success be? How will you know the process is working?

- What are the risks of the changes you contemplate? Can they be eliminated or minimized?

Implementation and evaluation: making things happen

Implementation

1. What should be the implementation process for each goal? How will all of the actions be connected?

2. Who will bear primary responsibility for implementation—the faculty as a whole? a specific subgroup of the faculty? the head or principal? a specific administrator?

3. What are obstacles to implementation?

4. Where is the leverage for overcoming obstacles?

5. What resources will be needed? How will you get them?

6. What is the timetable for implementation? How can you be realistic yet ambitious?

7. In what way will the implementers be held accountable?

8. How will you ensure that implementation is true to the spirit of each goal?

9. How will time be made available to those who must do the work?

10. How will momentum be maintained? How can you celebrate and sustain progress?

11. How will the community cope with change?

12. Who will provide positive reinforcement?

13. If the implementation process suggests changes in original goals, will a group or the individual responsible be able to change them?

14. Will someone be responsible for written description of the curriculum plan (mission statement, catalogue, student handbook, faculty handbook, course guides, other promotional literature)?

15. How will you publicize what you are doing to your external constituencies? How will you deal with disagreement?

16. What changes have already occurred as you went through the process?

17. Can or should change occur on an experimental or "pilot" basis?

18. How can you test your ideas without full-scale implementation?

19. How have you worked to ensure that the implementers are "invested" in the new curriculum?

20. How will you ensure that implementation honors the idea of the curriculum as hypothesis and teachers as research and development teams?

Evaluation

1. What provisions have been made for continuous reassessment, curriculum review, and planning?

2. How will you make sure of really seeing unanticipated results?

3. What worked the way you expected it would? What didn't? Why?

4. What did you forget, overlook, not understand?

5. How will you include students in evaluating the changes?

6. How will you include parents, board members, and others?

7. Would outside help be useful in gauging success?

8. What outside indicators would be helpful? What outside indicators will be unavoidable, even though not helpful?

9. Are there other ways to implement that might have better achieved the goal? Does this suggest adjustments now?

10. What has changed in the school? What new, unforeseen factors have developed that affected outcomes?

11. How dependent is the new curriculum on specific people? How can you institutionalize the changes to avoid this dependence?

12. How well have you provided for training newcomers and sustaining those who are doing the work?

13. What are your new null curriculum and your new hidden curriculum?

14. How can you really tell if outcomes and expectations are congruent?

15. What additional training is needed to support implementation?

16. To what extent do your professional development and evaluation systems link with and support curricular change?

17. How can you value and build on success and mistakes?

Resources

The resources that follow are included for guidance and food for thought as you approach the exciting challenge of a curriculum review. We encourage you to use them to provide fresh perspective, to expand your repertoire of ideas about curriculum, or to lend support to your existing beliefs. We believe that familiarity with the knowledge base surrounding curriculum is crucial to effective review (see Chapter 6, "Broadening Horizons").

We have listed books, journals, professional organizations, and government agencies, adding addresses and telephone numbers where appropriate. We chose to not list articles; there are simply too many.

This list, obviously idiosyncratic, in no way represents a comprehensive bibliography of curriculum; such a bibliography would be endless. Those who wish to look further or deeper will have no trouble finding leads.

The one criterion for inclusion was that someone on the NAIS Academic Services Committee had to have read the book and found it both readable and useful. Inclusion of a particular resource does not imply endorsement of a that point of view; we encourage you to consider many perspectives.

The books are grouped in four categories: curriculum content, curriculum implementation, diversity and gender issues in curriculum, and curriculum theory and moral climate.

BOOKS

Curriculum content

Adler, Mortimer, *A Guidebook to Learning.* New York: Macmillan, 1986.

An interesting discussion, based on the work done for the new *Encyclopaedia Britannica*, of the ways knowledge can be conceptualized and categorized. An appendix provides a compelling and useful outline for thinking about the issues of completeness and inclusion/exclusion in the high school curriculum.

Brandt, Ronald S., ed., *Content of the Curriculum.* Alexandria, Va.: Association for Supervision and Curriculum Development, 1988.

An outline of discipline-specific concepts—useful because this outline can be revised to respond to a variety of needs.

Bruner, Jerome, *The Process of Education.* Cambridge, Mass.: Harvard University Press, 1960.

In this landmark work of the curriculum reform movement of the 1960's, curriculum content includes "methods of disciplined inquiry, the development of logical processes, and the structure of the disciplines." Bruner believes that "the foundations of any subject may be taught to anybody at any age in some form."

Fenwick, James J., ed., *Caught in the Middle: Educational Reform for Young Adolescents in California Public Schools.* Sacramento, Calif.: Bureau of Publications, California State Department of Education, n.d.

This work of a task force of California educators, presented in highly usable form, covers every facet of middle school education. The first of the five sections is devoted to curriculum.

Finks, Harry, *Middle School Handbook.* Boston: National Association of Independent Schools, 1990.

Fast reading, with solid suggestions for the "care and feeding" of a middle school. Two chapters deal with curriculum and related issues.

Hirsch, E.D., Jr., *Cultural Literacy: What Every American Needs To Know.* Boston: Houghton Mifflin, 1987.

This book is a list containing information with which the author feels every American should be familiar, suggesting that it be the basis of a curriculum that would produce an educated America. More recently, he has produced a dictionary explaining all the items listed.

Papert, Seymour, *Mind-Storms.* New York: Basic Books, 1980.

This discussion of LOGO and computers has behind it philosophical ideas that challenge the way we think about readiness and about scope and sequence. Papert encourages educators to be anthropologists and to pay attention to the "cultural materials" available to the child's intellectual development.

Curriculum implementation

Bradley, Leo H., *Curriculum Leadership and Development Handbook.* Englewood Cliffs, N.J.: Prentice-Hall, 1985.

This practical resource gives step-by-step guidelines and materials for bringing about successful curriculum change and development.

Connelly, F. Michael, and D. Jean Clandinin, *Teachers as Curriculum Planners: Narratives of Experience.* New York: Teachers College Press, 1988.

Written for teachers and drawing heavily on the stories of teachers, this book affirms the central role of teachers in curriculum planning and supports those efforts.

Doll, Ronald C., *Curriculum Improvement: Decision Making and Process.* Boston: Allyn and Bacon, 1982.

Although the simulation exercises give it a textbook tone, this standard guide remains a ready and useful resource for planning curriculum change.

English, Fenwick W., and John C. Hill, *Restructuring: The Principal and Curriculum Change.* Reston, Va.: National Association of Secondary School Principals, 1990.

This small book can be read quite quickly. Its value is in its practical strategies for those responsible for guiding curriculum change in schools.

Fisher, Roger, and William I. Ury, *Getting to Yes: Negotiating Agreement without Giving In.* New York: Penguin Books, 1983.

Do not let the corporate-sounding title dissuade you from taking a look at this excellent guide to avoiding or getting through impasses that seem to have no resolution.

Glatthorn, Allan A., *Curriculum Renewal.* Alexandria, Va.: Association for Supervision and Curriculum Development, 1987.

Most usable by those who have some familiarity with curriculum terminology, this book is a succinct and exceptionally practical guide to planning curriculum projects.

Goodlad, John I., and associates, *Curricular Inquiry: The Study of Curriculum Practice.* New York: McGraw-Hill, 1979.

This study of curriculum practice includes an ordered view of the many domains of curriculum.

Gress, James R., and David Purpel, *Curriculum: An Introduction to the Field.* Berkeley, Calif.: McCutchan, 1978.

A valuable collection of essays on all aspects of curriculum.

Kaufman, R., *Identifying and Solving Problems: A Systems Approach,* 3rd ed. La Jolla, Calif.: University Associates, 1982.

To be used with any curricular models; a method of "needs assessment" to identify the gap between present conditions and desired educational goals.

Orenstein, Allan C., and Francis P. Hunkins, *Curriculum: Foundations, Principles and Issues.* Englewood Cliffs, N.J.: Prentice-Hall, 1988.

This text in curriculum foundations provides an overview of theory and implementation.

Saphier, Jon, et al., *How To Make Decisions That Stay Made.* Alexandria, Va.: Association for Supervision and Curriculum Development, 1989.

A short, useful book about good decision making.

Diversity and gender issues in curriculum

Abrams, Eileen, *A Curriculum Guide to Women's Studies for the Middle School, Grades 5-9.* Old Westbury, New York: The Feminist Press, 1986.

   This annotated bibliography focusing on academic subject content is a practical resource for those interested in adding a feminist balance to the curriculum.

Banks, James, *Teaching Strategies for Ethnic Studies.* Boston: Allyn and Bacon, 1987.

   A valuable resource of concepts, strategies, and materials for creating a truly inclusive curriculum.

Belenky, Mary Field, et al., *Women's Ways of Knowing.* New York: Basic Books, 1986.

   An important discussion of the ways women construct and articulate knowledge. The last chapters are particularly useful.

Chapman, Anne, *The Difference It Makes: A Resource Book on Gender for Educators.* Boston: National Association of Independent Schools, 1988.

   This excellent book on gender in education will prove very useful for anyone involved in curriculum and pedagogy.

Gilligan, Carol, *In A Different Voice.* Cambridge, Mass.: Harvard University Press, 1982.

   Probably the most important scholarly work to date on gender differences and the development of women.

Gilligan, Carol, ed., *Making Connections: The Relational Worlds of Adolescent Girls at Emma Willard School.* Cambridge, Mass.: Harvard University Press, 1990.

   Described as "a series of exercises en route to a new psychology of adolescence and women," this collection of essays is provocative and relevant to any discussion of curriculum.

McIntosh, Peggy, "Interactive Phases of Curricular Revision." Working Paper No. 124. Wellesley, Mass.: Wellesley College Center for Research on Women, 1983.

A touchstone for those beginning to widen the curriculum to include female learning styles and the concept of collaborative learning, this paper discusses the changes and conflicts through which a school can expect to go as it moves toward a more culturally diverse curriculum.

Minnich, Elizabeth Kamarck, *Transforming Knowledge.* Philadelphia: Temple University Press, 1990.

A provocative and beautifully written and argued book about transforming the curriculum of higher education to eliminate race, gender, and class bias. The first thirty pages are an extraordinary review of the evolution of inclusive thought.

Simonson, Rick and Scott Walker, eds., *Multi-Cultural Literacy: Opening the American Mind.* Saint Paul, Minn.: Graywolf Press, 1988.

Essays that underscore the importance of getting beyond Eurocentrism.

Sleeter, Christine, and Carl A. Grant, *Making Choices for Multicultural Education.* Columbus, Ohio: Merrill, 1988.

This compilation of critiques and reviews of over 200 articles and sixty books on multicultural education allows readers to select the best strategies for their specific needs.

Curriculum theory and moral climate

Adler, Mortimer, *The Paideia Proposal: An Educational Manifesto.* New York, Macmillan, 1982.

Adler presents his provocative, classical vision of good education. (A number of "paideia" schools have come into being around the country.)

Beyer, Landon E., and Michael W. Apple, eds., *The Curriculum: Problems, Politics and Possibilities.* Albany: SUNY Press, 1988.

This series of essays aims at reintegrating the ethical, personal, and political into curriculum discourse and decision making and succeeds in its aim. It is thoughtfully challenging of much that we take for granted in curriculum development and evaluation.

Bloom, Allan, *The Closing of the American Mind.* New York: Simon & Schuster, 1987.

This overview and analysis of the intellectual trends of our century would help engender philosophical discussion for those considering curriculum revision.

Bryk, Anthony, ed., "The Moral Life of Schools," vol. 96, no. 2, of the *American Journal of Education.* Chicago: University of Chicago Press, 1988.

The individual articles and the journal as a whole include extensive bibliographies of works past and current that are shifting educators' thinking about education for "goodness."

Dewey, John, *Experience and Education.* New York: Macmillan, 1939.

Dewey calls passionately for "a curriculum that poses problems rooted within the present experience and capacity of learners, problems that arouse an active quest for information and invite the production of new ideas."

Eisner, Elliot W., and Elizabeth Vallance, eds., *Conflicting Conceptions of Curriculum.* Berkeley, Calif.: McCutchan, 1974.

The editors provide essays to identify the assumptions underlying five common curricular orientations: cognitive process, technology, self-actualization, social reconstruction, and academic rationalism. The book is a kind of "map" of important curricular issues.

Gardner, Howard, *Frames of Mind: The Theory of Multiple Intelligences.* New York: Basic Books, 1983.

An excellent source for thinking about human development in diverse cultures as well as for expanding one's view of what constitutes intelligence. Each of the eight intelligences suggests its own approach to curriculum and pedagogy.

Gardner, John, *On Leadership.* New York: Free Press, 1989

An outstanding book on what leaders of all kinds need to be and do.

Resources

Goodlad, John I., ed., *The Ecology of School Renewal.* Chicago: National Society for the Study of Education and University of Chicago Press, 1987.

Chapters 1 and 12 are of particular interest in this NSSE yearbook. Chapter 1 gives a useful list of assumptions for curriculum improvements. Chapter 12 gives a well thought out description of a healthy school—the ultimate goal of any curriculum review.

Jackson, Philip W., "The Mimetic and the Transformative: Alternate Outlooks on Teaching," chapter 6 in *The Practice of Teaching.* New York: Teachers College Press, 1986.

The author defines the "mimetic" tradition as giving a central place to the transmission of factual and procedural knowledge through an imitative process. The "transformative" tradition seeks to accomplish some kind of qualitative change in the person being taught. This chapter explores the tangles that result when these traditions are not clearly understood or articulated in curriculum.

Jones, Richard M., *Fantasy and Feeling in Education.* New York: Harper and Row, 1968.

This essay uses a critique of Jerome Bruner's Man: A Course of Study as a basis for developing ideas about a "curriculum of emotions"— a challenging concept.

Levine, Sarah, *Promoting Adult Growth in Schools.* Boston: Allyn and Bacon, 1989.

A masterful look at the necessity of respecting teachers as adults who, because of the kind of work they do, grow as professionals as they mature as human beings.

Maeroff, Gene, *The Empowerment of Teachers.* New York: Teachers College Press, 1988.

An excellent study emphasizing the importance of teachers assuming the central role in all aspects of educating students. Readers concerned about the connotations of "empowerment" should not neglect this book.

Postman, Neil, and Charles Weingartner, *Teaching as a Subversive Activity,* New York: Dell, 1969.

This classic, well worth another look, says that sequential curriculum is useless because students do not learn in a sequential manner.

Powell, Arthur G., Eleanor Farrar, and David Cohen, *The Shopping Mall High School.* Boston: Houghton Mifflin, Boston, 1985.

The second report from A Study of High Schools details how high schools have created structures that create winners and losers and suggests ways for committed educators to increase the likelihood that all students will be well served.

Sizer, Theodore R., *Horace's Compromise: The Dilemma of the American High School.* Boston: Houghton Mifflin, 1984.

The author calls for focused curriculum and the empowerment of teachers in local high schools to stimulate effective education. This first report from A Study of High Schools served as the starting point for the Coalition of Essential Schools.

Stephens, J. M., *The Process of Schooling.* New York: Holt, Rinehart and Winston, 1967.

This study by an educational psychologist at the University of British Columbia challenges a number of common assumptions about what factors affect success in schools and develops a "theory of spontaneous schooling"—a useful counterpoint as we develop elaborate systems of curriculum and instruction.

Stone, Susan, *Strategic Planning for Independent Schools.* Boston: National Association of Independent Schools, 1987.

An excellent guide to good planning of all kinds.

Tyler, Ralph W., *Basic Problems of Curriculum and Instruction.* Chicago: University of Chicago Press, 1974 edition.

Tyler is an important voice in the evolution of the school of "positivism"—the assumption that real learning is that which can be demonstrated and evaluated with specific goals and objectives. Curriculum is the vehicle for achieving these specific ends.

Whitehead, Alfred North, *The Aims of Education.* New York: Macmillan, 1929.

This classic describes the interdependence of learning and calls for the elimination of departmentalization.

PROFESSIONAL ASSOCIATIONS

The professional associations listed here publish journals, sponsor conferences that deal with curriculum issues, or both. Recent important curriculum studies from four of the associations are also given.

American Association for the Advancement of Science
1333 H St., NW, Washington DC 20005
(202) 326-6400
Science for All Americans, 1989

American Council on the Teaching of Foreign Languages
6 Executive Plaza, Yonkers NY 10701
(914) 963-8830

American Educational Research Association
1201 16th St., NW, Washington DC 20036
(202) 223-9485

American Forum on Foreign Language and International Studies
49 W. 38th St., Suite 1500, New York NY 10018
(212) 732-8606

Association for Supervision and Curriculum Development
1250 N. Pitt St., Alexandria VA 22314
(703) 549-9110

Bradley Commission on History in the Schools
26915 Westwood Rd., Suite A-2, Westlake OH 44145
(216) 835-1776
Building a History Curriculum: Guidelines for Teaching History in the Schools

Coalition of Essential Schools
Box 1938, Brown University, Providence RI 02912
(401) 863-3384

College Board, Academic Preparation Series
45 Columbus Ave., New York NY 10023
(212) 713-8000

Council for Basic Education
725 15th St. NW, Washington DC 20005
(202) 347-4171

Educational Leadership Institute, Inc.
P.O. Box 863, Springfield MA 01101
(413) 736-6990

Getty Center for Education in the Arts (J. Paul Getty Trust)
1875 Century Park East, Suite 2300, Los Angeles CA 90067
(213) 277-9188

International Reading Association
800 Barksdale Road, Box 8139, Newark DE 19714
(302) 731-1600

Music Educators National Conference
1902 Association Drive, Reston VA 22091
(703) 860-4000

National Art Education Association
1916 Association Drive, Reston VA 22091
(703) 860-8000

National Association for the Education of Young Children
1834 Connecticut Ave. NW, Washington DC 20009
(202) 232-8777

National Association of Independent Schools
75 Federal St., Boston MA 02110
(617) 451-2444

National Association of Secondary School Principals
1904 Association Drive, Reston VA 22091
(703) 860-0200

National Council for the Social Studies
3501 Newark St. NW, Washington DC 20016
(202) 960-7840

National Council of Teachers of English
1111 Kenyon Rd., Urbana IL 61801
(217) 328-3870
The English Coalition Conference: Democracy through Language

National Council of Teachers of Mathematics
1906 Association Drive, Reston VA 22091
(703) 620-9840
Curriculum and Evaluation Standards for School Mathematics

National Middle School Association
4807 Evanswood Dr., Columbus OH 43229-6292
(614) 848-8211

National Science Teachers Association
1742 Connecticut Avenue NW, Washington DC 20009
(202) 328-5800

The National Society for the Study of Education
5835 Kimbark Ave., Chicago IL 60637
(312) 702-1582

GOVERNMENT- ASSOCIATED AGENCIES AND INSTITUTES

ERIC (Educational Resources Information Center)
4833 Rugby Ave., Suite 301, Bethesda MD 20814
(301) 656-9723
(Access through DIALOG computer software)

Appalachia Educational Laboratory
P.O. Box 1348, Charleston WV 25325
(304) 347-0400

Far West Laboratory for Educational Research and Development
1855 Folsom St., San Francisco CA 94103
(415) 565-3000

Mid-Continent Regional Educational Laboratory
12500 East Iliff Ave., Suite 201, Aurora CO 80014
(303) 337-0990

National Diffusion Network
555 New Jersey Ave., Washington DC 20208
(202) 357-6140

North Central Regional Educational Laboratory
295 Emroy Ave., Elmhurst IL 60126
(708) 941-7677

The Regional Laboratory for Educational Improvement
290 S. Main St., Andover MA 01810
(508) 470-0098

Northwest Regional Educational Laboratory
101 SW Main St., Suite 500, Portland OR 97204
(503) 275-9500

Research for Better Schools
444 N. Third St., Philadelphia PA 19123
(215) 574-9300

Southeastern Educational Improvement Laboratory
P.O. Box 12746
200 Park Ave., Suite 203, Research Triangle Park NC 27709
(919) 549-8216

Southwest Educational Development Laboratory
211 E. Seventh St., Austin TX 78701
(512) 476-6861

SWRL Educational Research and Development
4665 Lampson Ave., Los Alamitos CA 90720
(213) 598-7661